St Mary's Cathedral Wrexham

The Story of a Catholic Community

Kathryn Byrne

St Mary's Cathedral, Wrexham — the story of a Catholic Community
First published in Wales in 2007
by
BRIDGE BOOKS
61 Park Avenue
Wrexham
Ll12 7AW

ISBN: 978-1-84494-042-4

A catalogue record for this book is available from the British Library

Printed and bound in China by

CTPS

To my husband

Rev. Patrick Byrne (Deacon)
1936–2002

Who will be so pleased that I have completed it.

St Mary's Cathedral, Wrexham. [Dr Matthew Byrne]

Contents

Acknowledgements

I would like to thank everyone who has helped in any way with this book. I wish to thank Tom Parker for his work on my behalf at Clifton Diocesan Archives. I would like to note my appreciation of the memoirs of the late Frank More whose notes were invaluable in building up a picture of the 1920s and 1930s. I would like to thank those former Convent girls who shared their memories with me over a pleasant lunch. My sincere thanks to Dr Kathryn Ellis of NEWI for reading the final manuscript.

I also wish to thank my brother-in-law, Dr Matthew Byrne, FRPS, for taking the beautiful photographs of the Cathedral building, and the Abbot of Downside, Dom Aidan Bellinger, OSB, for allowing me to use the portraits of the Vicars Apostolic from his book *Fathers in Faith*. Thanks are also due to Denbighshire Record Office for allowing me to reproduce the item on page 32. My thanks also to Dr Mary braid for copies of photographs collected in the parish. I wish also to thank the staff of Wrexham Library and Arts Centre and the A. N. Palmer Centre, Wrexham, for all their help in seeking out information on my behalf.

Foreword

by

Rt Revd Edwin Regan
Bishop of Wrexham

Any people who do not know, or forget, their history are deprived. If we realise our story, we can appreciate better our present gifts, and draw inspiration for the future from those who have gone before us. We stand on their shoulders!

Kathryn Byrne has revealed to us the amazing and moving story of the Catholic Faith in Wrexham since the Reformation. Wales has been a Catholic country for most of its recorded history – Catholics have been in the minority for only 500 years. During the first thousand years of Christianity in this land, Wales belonged to the Catholic Church as she developed down the centuries.

Sometimes we think that our Catholic story began when bishops and dioceses were restored in 1850; this book will help us to appreciate our roots.

We have a message to give to modern Wales – the message of the Good News of Jesus Christ, lived and celebrated in the Catholic Church.

We rejoice that we share so much of this Good News with our fellow Christians, and wish to walk with them in every way that is acceptable. However, we believe that the Catholic Church is singular since She alone has preserved that unity around Peter which is Christ's gift to His Church. Our Catholic story has a chapter that speaks of Welsh martyrs who sacrificed their lives rather than deny the primacy of the Bishop of Rome. This cloud of unseen witnesses urges us today to live a life of Faith worthy of their sacrifice.

I pray that our Catholic story will inspire us to write the next chapter aglow with the Spirit of Christ, 'so that a people yet unborn may praise the Lord'.

CHAPTER ONE

The Old Order Passes Away ...

The church of Our Lady of Sorrows, now the cathedral church of the Roman Catholic Diocese of Wrexham and a Grade II listed building, has stood in Regent Street for 150 years. It was built in 1857, at the height of the revival of the Roman Catholic Church in Britain. At this time, it was recovering from 300 years of persecution, since the period of religious changes in the sixteenth century, which came to be known as the Reformation. What follows is a glimpse into the story of Catholics in Wrexham from the sixteenth century until today.

Long known as a Protestant town, celebrating the memory of Walter Cradock and Morgan Llwyd, it is easy to forget that until the sixteenth century upheavals, Wrexham's townsfolk would have been Catholic.

On the eve of the Reformation, the town of Wrexham was very much smaller than we know it today. It was also much more rural. Described as 'the only market town in Walshe Maylor',[1] it was famous for its great March Fair, to which traders came from all over north Wales and across the border in England. An important marketing centre since the Middle Ages, it offered a variety of goods for sale — livestock, dairy produce, linen, woollen goods, leather, lead and ironware. At the heart of this bustling town stood the Parish Church of St Giles, whose bells summoned Wrexham people to Mass and other religious ceremonies.

On the eve of the Reformation, there is no evidence to suggest a desire for church reform on the part of Wrexham people and there seems to have been no unrest of a religious kind. Money was still being left in wills for the repose of the donors' souls, a practice later to be suppressed by Protestants. It seems too that Wrexham people were proud of their church, leaving bequests for its upkeep and where work on the tower, the church's crowning glory and a wonder of Wales, was nearing completion at this time. There was even talk of St Giles church becoming the cathedral of the diocese.

Church life in Wrexham at this time was, most likely, typical of any town in the kingdom, popular, vibrant and very much alive. Wrexham people would have found in St Giles, a place where the Christian message touched all of the senses — touch and smell, as well as sight and hearing. Its statues, stained glass, paintings, the incense, the blessing of candles at Candlemas, the palms on Palm Sunday, the Corpus Christi processions, the religious guilds and confraternities, the cult of saints, relics, pilgrimages and at the centre, the Mass — all fitting into the seasons of the year and the Church's calendar — helped to raise the people's minds and hearts to God. Furthermore, Wrexham people would have felt at home with the familiar Latin of the Mass and other ceremonies as well as with the clergy and churchwardens who were nearly all as Welsh as themselves.

At a national level too, there was acceptance and even some pleasure in Wales to have Henry VIII as their king. When his father, the first Tudor king, ascended the throne, no part

TOWER . WREXHAM . 30120 . J.V.

of Britain had welcomed him more than Wales, for he was seen as a fulfilment of the bardic prophecies of a Welsh king on the English throne.

There was no indication then, that most of what was familiar about the Church was on the threshold of great change. We need to ask how it could be that the great medieval Church, which had been a pervasive presence in people's lives for centuries could, within a few decades, come toppling down. There were several reasons.

The early sixteenth century was a time of great change — socially, culturally and economically. The church was seen as having great wealth and power beyond her calling for the salvation of people's souls through the celebration of Mass and the sacraments. Also, a characteristic of the age was its sheer materialism and desire for wealth affecting particularly those who held power in the land, Henry VIII among them.

Furthermore, there was a lack of those high ideals characteristic of the ages of faith, so that when the Church was challenged, it was only rare exceptions like Thomas More, John Fisher and the martyrs who retained those ideals. There had also developed an attitude of obedience and submission to the King and so when Henry broke with the See of Rome in 1531, declaring himself 'Supreme Head of the English Church', it opened the way for the changes which were to follow.

Perhaps the first inkling that Wrexham people had that the old order was about to change was when they heard in 1536 that nearby Valle Crucis Abbey, which had strong links with Wrexham, had been dissolved and its monks pensioned off. A poor, small house compared with many of the abbeys in England, it was in decline, its monks having dwindled to a pitiful few. There seems to have been no protest at its passing. Its closure saw the end of what has been described as 'at its best, an illustrious chapter in the history of religion in Wales.'[2]

On the continent, Luther and other reformers had seen the need for renewal in the church, as there always is. They wanted a simplification and purification of the Christian faith and they undertook to reform religion on the basis of Scripture and the early church, seeing superstition in many of the religious practices of the time. They wanted every Christian to be able to read the Bible in his or her mother tongue. Copies of the Scriptures were now more readily available through the invention of printing half a century before.

The Acts of Union of 1535, 1536 and 1543 linked Wales more closely to England and from that time on, Wales was governed by English laws and English was to be the official language. Increasingly, young Welsh men went to Oxford and Cambridge universities. Some of them returned as supporters of the new learning and inspired with the ideas of the Protestant Reformation.

The middle decades of the sixteenth century must have been a time of confusion and uncertainty for many, as with each change of monarch, religious policy swung to and fro. We know that the Vicar of Wrexham, Hugh Puleston, retained his position throughout this period, receiving increasing honours in the Church as time went by and undoubtedly bending this way and that to the winds of change when they came — a veritable Vicar of Bray.

Even more change came with the accession of Edward VI, Henry's son, when the new reforming ideas began to take hold. By the late 1540s there was a minority in Wales devoutly

Facing: The Parish Church of St Giles, Wrexham, completed in 1520, just before the advent of the Reformation, the last Catholic Church to be built in Wrexham for four hundred years. [W. Alister Williams Collection]

attached to them. One of these was William Salesbury, a Denbighshire man, who had come into contact with Protestant ideas while at Oxford University and the Inns of Court. He realised that if Wales was to become Protestant, it should have both a Bible and a Prayer Book in the Welsh language. 'The word of God' he said in 1551, 'is bound in fetters'.[3] In Elizabeth's reign he was to translate part of the New Testament into Welsh. Nevertheless, by the end of Edward's reign, Wales could still in no way be said to be a Protestant country, although it is thought that some of the towns which were to become firmly Puritan in the seventeenth century, had the seeds of the new faith sown at this time. One such town is said to have been Wrexham.

In general, people were too attached to the old ways and Edward's reforms were seen to be more drastic and less acceptable than those of his father. In the six years of his reign, all the ancient ceremonies of the Old Church disappeared. The new Book of Common Prayer was required by law to be used and church services were to be in English, even in Wales. The cult of saints, relics and pilgrimages, the blessing of candles at Candlemas and palms on Palm Sunday were all forbidden. Altars, stained glass, paintings and statues in church were either removed, defaced or covered in limewash. In 1549, the Mass was outlawed, completing the radical transformation of the Church, which had been a pervasive presence in people's lives for over a thousand years.

All of this would have affected Wrexham's church of St Giles and further changes were in store for the Vicar of Wrexham and his flock, when, after the early death of Edward VI, his sister, Mary, came to the throne in 1553. She had remained a Catholic. Support for her in Wales was stronger than in any other part of the kingdom, although she was probably welcomed as their own Welsh princess, rather than for her Catholic beliefs. In north Wales, she was proclaimed Queen both at Beaumaris and Denbigh and was greeted with affection by several Welsh poets.

Mary had two aims — to produce a Catholic male heir and to bring her country back to the Catholic faith. She said that she had no intention of compelling or constraining men's consciences, although she set about restoring the Catholic faith. Catholic worship and practices were reintroduced in piecemeal fashion in both England and Wales. The Latin Mass was restored. In the parishes, orders were received to paint the churches and to carve new rood screens to replace those so recently discarded. Despite the expense, this seems to have been carried out, and quite quickly. In general, there seems to have been little resistance to Mary's reinstatement of the Catholic Church.

We do not know the views of the people of Wrexham or even their vicar, but whatever his views, he complied with the new order of things. In any case the English liturgy enforced under Edward, would have held very little appeal for the Welsh, and many must have resented the fact that their churches had been stripped of everything beautiful.

In 1555, Mary revived the medieval laws against heresy, intending to make an example of just a few heretics. But by the end of her reign, 273 people had died for the Protestant cause, although perhaps it is significant that there were none in north Wales.[4]

Queen Mary and her archbishop, Cardinal Reginald Pole, were soon to set in motion Catholic reforms inspired by the recent Council of Trent. In Wales, Thomas Goldwell, Bishop of St Asaph, under whose charge Wrexham came, and gifted writers like Morys Clynnog and Gruffudd Roberts, made a determined effort to introduce the ideals of the Catholic Reformation into Wales. But this restoration of the Catholic Church was short-lived. Mary died in 1558, and was succeeded by Elizabeth. By this time however, it is said that the foundations of any later Welsh Catholic opposition to Protestantism had been laid.

On the accession of Elizabeth, it soon became clear that her aim was political unity both within the country and in matters of religion. She would allow only one church and that the reformed one as in Edward's day. In an attempt to wipe out Catholicism, more and more laws were enacted against those still adhering to the Old Faith. Although not always strictly enforced, fines were imposed for non-attendance at church. The mere threat was sufficient to encourage most people to conform.

Yet, despite the laws, many Catholics still clung to their faith during this time. Pockets of Catholics in north Wales, centred on the houses of leading families, such as the Edwardses of Chirk or in Holywell, the major centre of Catholicism in north Wales. Some people from Wrexham and elsewhere might have travelled to either place to a Mass, said in secret, sometimes at dead of night. But for the most part, the Welsh Catholics were neglected, for want of priests. Some of these still clung on to Catholic practices, such as praying at gravesides or making the sign of the cross, which gradually over the years lost their meaning and some suggest that they were not to be truly Protestantized until the Methodist Revival.[5]

Meanwhile, Catholic England and Wales became a church on the run and while those clinging to the Old Faith faced fines, forfeiture of land, imprisonment and even execution, some escaped to the Continent, many eminent north Wales churchmen among them. It was here that the real vitality of the English (and Welsh) Catholic Church was to be found — in a church in exile. The importance of the exiles was soon to become out of all proportion to their numbers. Until the time of the French Revolution, continental Europe was to be a refuge for English and Welsh Catholic gentry and clergy. Seminaries, schools, monasteries and convents were founded, some of them remaining until recent times. In order to provide well-trained and zealous priests, a Lancashire priest, William Allen, set up a seminary at Douai in the Low Countries as it was forbidden by law to train priests in England or Wales. Its aim was to save the souls of their fellow-countrymen; it had no political agenda. It soon attracted over one hundred men, English and Welsh, both priests and students already scattered on the continent. Some of the early students included John Gruffydd (mentioned at the trial of Richard Gwyn and said to have worked in both the Ruabon area and in the Llŷn Peninsula). There was also John Bennett of Cwm, near Holywell, later to join Richard Gwyn in gaol and face torture. From the 1580s, he was to work among the 'poore and meaner sort of people' who flocked to him from around Holywell and various parts of north Wales'.[6] Both priests must surely have visited Wrexham.

In 1578, a further seminary for the training of priests was founded in Rome with Dr Morys Clynnog of Caernarfonshire as its first rector. It is thought that during Elizabeth's reign about one hundred men attended the continental seminaries. Seventy of these were ordained priests and over sixty were sent on the mission. Of these, seventeen came originally from the diocese of St Asaph and twelve from the diocese of Bangor, and between 1574 and 1578, eleven out of the fifty-two men ordained at Douai were Welsh.[7]

In 1570, Pope Pius V excommunicated Queen Elizabeth in his bull '*Regnans in excelsis*', but what the Pope failed to realise was that Elizabeth was a very popular Queen among Protestants and Catholics alike, especially in Wales on account of her Welsh blood. But further laws were enacted against Catholics and soon the papal cause became, in the English and Welsh mind, a threat to overthrow a very popular queen. Government propaganda from 1574 onwards saw all Catholics as potential rebels, ready to welcome an invasion by a foreign power. It was at this time that a list of influential Catholic laymen in the country was drawn up.[8] Eleven of these were from north Wales and included John Edwards of Chirk, ten miles from Wrexham. For three generations the Edwards family of Plas Newydd, Chirk, remained Roman Catholics, upholding the Catholic cause in the area.

But the government had some grounds for its fears. Catholics were beginning to grow in both numbers and zeal after the first priests arrived from the seminary at Douai. And the character of Catholicism was changing. There were plans afoot to replace Elizabeth on the throne by Mary, Queen of Scots, while during the years 1575 and 1576, Dr Morys Clynnog, probably backed by Owen Lewis, put forward a plan to invade the country and secure it for Catholicism. Writing to the Pope, he asked him to equip a fleet which was to 'make a landing in the remoter parts of England, which the Cymry or the Welsh inhabit today' (i.e. Wales). The plan was to restore the Queen of Scots 'to her rightful position in England'. He thought an invasion through Wales would be welcomed 'the Welsh ... being most devoted to the Catholic faith'.[9]

Seminary priests had been coming into the area from the College in Douai from 1574 onwards and their influence was beginning to be felt.

Meanwhile, those Catholics not attending the services of the new State Church were coming under greater scrutiny. In October 1577, the bishops were given directions to report the situation in their dioceses. However, William Hughes, Bishop of St Asaph, reported 'none in his diocese who refuse or neglect to come to church'.[10] Nevertheless, Holywell's Well of St Winefride, in his diocese, was continuing to attract Catholics. He was clearly considered lax. The appointment of John Whitgift, Bishop of Worcester, as Vice-President of the Council of the Marches reflected more accurately the anxiety of the Privy Council. He had a reputation for being a strict disciplinarian and a keen anti-Romanist.

In February 1578, a commission was granted to the bishop of St Asaph 'for the triall of certen persons within the counties of Flint and Denbigh detected of hearing Masses and using other supersticions contrarie to the present state of religion'.[11]

Fearful by now of the effect of the seminary priests, the Council of the Marches at Ludlow, referred in a letter of 1579 to 'certain evil disposed persons being sent from Rome and termed reconcilers to have crept among her highness subjects ... and seduced many of them from the true religion established in this realm'. They pointed to Chirk and Holywell as centres of recusancy, giving instructions to Sir Henry Sidney, Lord President of the Council of Wales and the Marches 'to enquire into those disorders'.[12] The Acts of the Privy Council, 1578–82, give further evidence of the presence of Catholic recusants at this time. In a letter to the Bishop of Worcester (Vice-President of the Council), they point to 'disorders in the house of John Edwardes of Cherk ... towching Papistrie'.[13]

Further letters reveal their continuing concern, until on 27 May 1582, they sent a letter saying 'Their Lordships doe perceive the number of Recusants to be verie much increased of late' and lay the blame firmly on the slackness 'of the Justices sheriffe and Jurors in sondrie of these counties (where) they have not been indicted and convicted according to the tenour of the Statute'.[14] Clearly the Justices, in the eyes of the Privy Council, had not been diligent enough in seeking out Catholics.

Meanwhile, John Edwards of Chirk was accused of inviting recusants to his house to hear Mass being said by the seminary priests. Fr. Edward Hughes was mentioned by name, though there were five priests there altogether. John Edwards' wife was also accused of going to Holywell to hear Mass on the feast of St Winefride.

Fr. Edward Hughes is also known to have said Mass in Erbistock and Pickhill, while John Gruffydd is described as being active in the Ruabon area, not far from Wrexham. Fr. John Bennett was to be another priest active in north Wales from about 1580 'travelinge Wales all over, especially the north part thereof'.[15] It is inconceivable that these priests did not visit Wrexham, the largest town in north Wales.

The times must have been very confusing for ordinary people. What had always been Catholic doctrine and practice had been outlawed under Edward, restored under Mary and now outlawed again under Elizabeth. Many must have gone to church completely bewildered at what was happening. As reign followed reign, fiercer and fiercer laws were to be enacted against Catholics. Only a few men and women would be brave enough to challenge the law of the land and to try to maintain Catholic belief and practices. Doing so, they would be facing the possibility of a fine at least and at worst, meet with a gruesome death. Lack of priests in Wales was to prove a major problem. Robert Persons, the Jesuit, wrote at this time that Wales was 'lapsed into dense ignorance about it [the Catholic religion] due to the lack of priests'. Perhaps he was unaware of what was being achieved. He recommended a mission to Wales, 'which was not so hostile to the Catholic religion'.[16]

Throughout the Elizabethan period both Catholic and Protestant writers commented on the Welsh remaining Catholic at heart. Yet despite the fierce laws, some young men continued to offer themselves to be priests. Richard and Francis Edwards, probably nephews of John Edwards of Chirk, went to the Continent to be educated as priests in 1581 and it is thought that between 1585 and 1593, twelve students left north Wales for continental seminaries.

Meanwhile, we know that there were a number of Catholics in Wrexham at this time. They are listed in the return of papists for Wrexham in 1581 as follows: Dame Margaret Atherton, wife of William Edwards Esq. (she was a Lancashire woman, who had taken William Edwards of Stansty as her second husband), Mary Tylsley (her maid), John Berse, Gwen *verch* Ellis (his wife), Margaret, Catherine and Jane (his daughters), Robert ap Evan

Plas Cadwgan, Bersham, the home of the recusant Edward Jones who was executed for his involvement in the Babington Plot to depose Elizabeth I and replace her on the throne with Mary Queen of Scots. It is likely that Catholic Masses were performed in the hall. [W. Alister Williams Collection]

and Thomas (his servants) and Richard Whyte (a prisoner). There were also Catholics in the districts around Wrexham, including seven at Bangor-on-Dee, three at Holt, two at Erbistock and two at Chirk.[17] Four years later, two leading gentlemen of the Wrexham area, Edward Jones of Plas Cadwgan and Edward Puleston of Hafod-y-Wern, were returned as recusants by the Wrexham churchwardens.[18] But there may have been many more who were not discovered.

Richard Whyte or Gwyn, listed as 'a prisoner' in 1581, is said to have acted as agent for priests in the area. It is said that he knew at least fifteen, a significant number. He was born at Llanidloes 'descended from honest parentage'.[19] He studied at Oxford for a time and then moved to Cambridge. He left university without a degree and became a schoolmaster at Overton-on-Dee. Later, he moved to Wrexham, then Gresford and Yswyd and returned to Overton, where he married 'a younge girle', Catharine. They had six children.[20]

As a convinced Catholic, Richard refused to receive communion in the Established Church. His name was among those presented to the Bishop of St Asaph for non-attendance at Divine Service in 1581.[21] The Privy Council stressed the need for the Welsh bishops to take action against 'all schoolmasters, public and private' and this eventually led to his persecution and arrest. Furthermore, he was acting as an agent for the priests coming over from the Continent.

Puritanism, meanwhile, had become strong and well-organised in this part of the country by the 1580s. Wrexham tradesmen such as David Edwards, a mercer, were influenced by Protestantism in the Chester area and tried to impose Calvinistic ideas on the parish church at Wrexham. The Puritans' enemies called them 'pedlars and tinkers, hot Puritans and full of the Gospel'.[22] Their zeal may account for the fact that Richard Gwyn met with persecution at Overton. So he moved to Erbistock, where he set up a school in a barn.

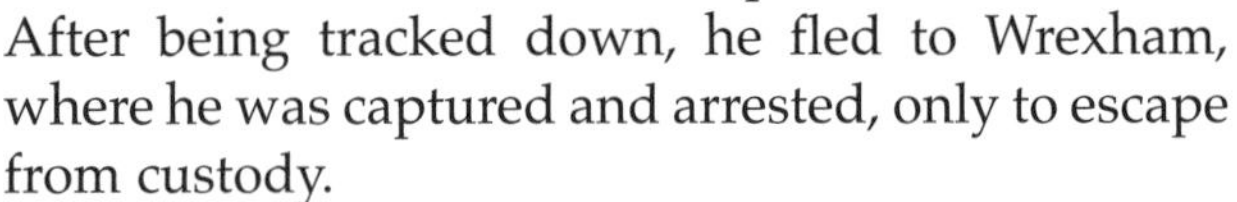

After being tracked down, he fled to Wrexham, where he was captured and arrested, only to escape from custody.

Richard Gwyn was a gifted man, thought to be 'inferior to none in his countrye in the Welshe tongue'[23] and the five '*Carolau*' or poems, which he has left to us, bear this out. They are free-metre poems, stressing the spiritual value of traditional Catholic belief and practice and the danger of the new Reformation ideas, as he saw them.

In July 1580, he was arrested and imprisoned in '*Y Siambr ddu*' (the black chamber) 'a vile and filthy prison'[24] under the Shirehall. From now on, he was moved from gaol to gaol and court to court in Wrexham, Denbigh and Holt, where he was 'endited of high treason'[25] for having tried to persuade someone from the religion established by law. He was then moved to Bewdley and Bridgnorth, where he and fellow-prisoners were

A sketch of St Richard Gwyn drawn by Canon Adolph Evans.

examined and tortured. He made a seventh appearance in court, this time in Wrexham, in the spring of 1584. His eighth and final appearance in court was again at Wrexham on 9 October 1584 when he was found guilty of a charge of treason and sentenced to death.

The Reliquary of St Richard Gwyn.

It is said that on the day of his execution, the Vicar of Wrexham asked him if he acknowledged the Queen to be 'supream head of the Church'. He answered, 'I acknowledge her to be lafell (i.e. lawful) queene of England and otherwise I never said.'[26]

He was executed at Wrexham's Beast Market on Thursday, 15 October 1584, by being hanged, drawn and quartered. It is said that people of all kinds were compelled to be present at the event. It says much for the people of Wrexham that a jury 'being called (at one of his many trials), not one of them would appear, although they were threatened by fines' and at his execution, 'the demeanour of the people was such that the executioner sheltered in a 'chamber close prisoner' for fear of his life. The ladder needed for the execution had to be stolen at midnight, while 'coles' had to be carried two miles from the pit 'for want of a hors' and an axe had to be taken from a butcher's stall.[27]

Perhaps Wrexham people were compassionate or perhaps they were still Catholic at heart and in sympathy with Richard Gwyn's views on the Reformation changes in the church. At any rate, the author of the Holywell MS recalled, 'The people knew his innocency, being well-acquainted with the good man's conversation ye space of Xxtie [20] years together.' They knew his cause to be just and honest, being directly for religion.[28] Richard Gwyn was canonised by Pope Paul VI on 25 October 1970 and his feastday is celebrated on 16 October. Before he died, Richard left gifts to fifteen priests known to him. That he knew so many priests personally is perhaps some indication of Catholic activity in the area at this time.

The life of these priests was very hard. They were trained to be self-reliant and they needed to be. They had none of the outward trappings usually associated with the life of a priest — priestly dress, a church, a hierarchy above or below. Always on the run, expecting at any time to be discovered, a priest had to survive, say Mass, baptise, marry, bury, preach and reconcile. He had to educate and encourage the laity. He had to find lodgings, be fed, be hidden and taken from point to point. John Edwards would have succoured many of the priests arriving in the area, either at Plas Newydd, Chirk, or at Plas-yn-y-Pentre, the former grange of Valle Crucis Abbey, which his family had acquired at the Dissolution. The presence in the house of secret passages, hiding holes, a hidden staircase and a false floor bear silent witness to those who tried to continue to practise their Catholic faith in the sixteenth century and beyond, at the risk of their lives.

The 1587 Act 'to retain the Queen's Majesty's subjects in due obedience' overhauled all the existing laws against Catholics. A recusant who did not pay the monthly fines could

gell & ti a vyddi well/oddiwrth
Val i trelia y tan gan bwyll//gwr
y ganwyll// gynnydd/ velly dy einoes dan y rrod/ sydd yn darvod/ bevnydd.·/ Nad ith lygeid vynd ynghy
//roi dy vryd// ar gysgv/ nes yt wneuthur vnion raith & am dy waith//
yn pechv//.·/ Gwrando gyngor gwr oth wlad// ti ai kai vo yn rrad// y Kymro/ yw vyfyrio or barth ir
Richard
Gwyn St.
I do forgive thee with all my heart God & our blessed Lady & St. Michael forgive thee

have all his goods and chattels taken and two-thirds of his lands seized. It is fair to say that the laws were not always carried out, but the threat of it ensured that only the most committed, bravest Catholics tried to continue to practise their faith. Many gave up at this time. It was, by and large, the wealthiest families which were able to carry on, hearing Mass in secret, sometimes at dead of night, paying the fines when necessary, facing imprisonment, torture and even death, while hoping for better times.

The Catholic Church became a domestic church, a priest saying Mass for the landed family and their servants, sometimes being retained as the family's chaplain, while being passed off as a tutor to their children or even a servant. Others simply moved on to the next big house. Meanwhile, a huge step, very dear to Welsh reformers, took place in 1588. It has been said that the great gift of the Reformation to Wales was the Welsh Bible. William Morgan undertook this great work single-handedly, while he was Vicar of Llanrhaiadr-ym-Mochnant, in the diocese of St Asaph. As well as bringing the Word of God to the people of Wales in their own tongue, it has had untold influence on the Welsh language, Welsh literature and Welsh thought from that day to this. It was later to play a most important part in the Methodist Revival.

By the 1590s, Catholicism seems to have been on the increase in north Wales. We might have expected that the fierce legislation of the 1580s would have stamped it out completely, both at home and abroad. It had not done so. There is some indication that Catholic recusants in Denbighshire formed part of this increase. Those presented as Catholic recusants in 1581 had been thirty-eight, and while it dipped in 1587 to thirteen, by 1592, forty-eight Denbighshire Catholics were convicted of recusancy.[29]

This trend was obviously giving concern to the authorities. In June 1592, the Privy Council asked the Earl of Pembroke to provide names of gentlemen in Wales 'sound in religion and well affected to Her Majesty and the state', so that they might be commissioned 'for inquiry of Jesuits, Seminaries and such lewd suspected persons as do lurk in those remote places'.[30]

Another letter at about this time abhorred the fact that large numbers of people in Wales were frequenting 'certain places where in times past there have been pilgrimages, images or offerings' and instructions followed for 'superstitious and idolatrous monuments to be pulled down, broken and quite defaced, so as there be no remnant, token or memory of the same.'[31] This must have referred to Holywell especially.

Nevertheless, Catholicism continued to grow in north Wales at this time, so that 'the Commissioners do not know what course to take to extinguish them', wrote the Catholic Richard Verstegan.[32] The course the government took was to yet again tighten up the laws. Despite this, well into the 1590s young men were still offering themselves for the priesthood. Between 1585 and 1593 about a dozen students from north Wales made their way to Continental seminaries, no doubt assisted by William Davies, a priest who was to meet his death as a result.[33] A poignant note can be seen in the diary of Douay College for 6 September 1598, 'There arrived here, William, son of Richard White [i.e. Richard Gwyn] … His father bravely met his death in 1584 in defence of the true faith'.[34]

As far as lay people are concerned, there is only one Catholic whom we know of in the Wrexham area at this date. This was Edward Puleston of Hafod-y-Wern, who was several

Facing: 'St Richard Gwyn – Welsh Martyr', an icon in St Mary's Cathedral by Sister Petra Clare.

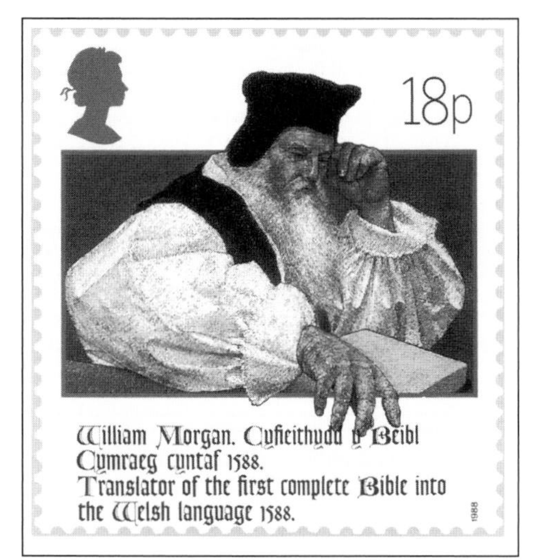

William Morgan, the Bishop of St Asaph, by Wrexham artist Keith Bowen.

times convicted of recusancy during the 1590s. He owed the Crown £100 for being absent from church for five lunar months.[35]

Elizabeth's reign was drawing to a close, when in 1602, she issued a proclamation against Catholic priests, stressing that her 'recent clemency' would cease. They were to depart the realm or the full severity of the law would operate against them.

On 2 July of the same year, William Morgan, Bishop of St Asaph, presented sixty-five people at the Denbighshire Great Sessions for not attending the Established Church during the previous twelve months. Of these, fifteen were from Wrexham, but we do not know whether they were Puritans, Catholics or a mixture of both.[36]

On 24 March 1603, Elizabeth died. Her attempts to unite the nation had not completely succeeded, but she had managed to unite the vast majority of people under the Anglican Church by the end of her reign. There were still English and Welsh Catholics both at home and abroad determined to hold on to the Old Faith and there were still young Welshmen going abroad to be educated as priests. At the other end of the scale were the Puritans, whose numbers had increased rapidly during her reign. Their day was to come.

The Catholics retained their belief in the real presence of Christ in the Eucharist, among the seven sacraments as a means of grace and the concept of the Universal Church, with the Pope as its visible head and authority. The Puritans, on the other hand, looked to the Bible as sole authority for divine truth, retaining only those sacraments mentioned in Scripture. The Book of Common Prayer provided for the Anglican liturgy. Catholics were increasingly to stress those aspects of the faith either played down or denied by the Protestant reformers and vice versa.

Although Catholicism was forbidden by law in Wales as in England, Wales by the beginning of the seventeenth century had not become fully Protestant. It was only a few, educated and privileged, who were fired by Reformation ideals. The rest had sunk into deep ignorance of the Christian faith. It is said that the Welsh were still Catholic at heart but, deprived of priests and so instruction, their faith was soon to descend into superstition. Some religious practices remained, but gradually they lost their meaning.

Despite the fact that between 1558 and 1603, fifty-four men in Wales alone went to be trained as Catholic priests, Catholicism was not to be restored. But vocations to the priesthood continued to come from those little pockets of Catholicism where the missionary priests had worked so hard. However, few of them were to return to their native land.[37]

In the whole of Wales, according to the Anglican bishops, there were 808 Catholic recusants by the end of the century; 250 of them in the St Asaph diocese.[38] It is likely that there were a few in Wrexham by the end of Elizabeth's reign — possibly some of the fifteen people presented for recusancy in 1602. However, it would be the Puritans of Wrexham who would exert most influence, in politics as much as religion, during the following decades.

References

1. LELAND, *Itinerary*.
2. WILLIAMS, Glanmor, *Wales and the Reformation*, UWP, 1999, p99.
3. Ibid, p235.
4. HUGHES, Philip, *The Reformation in England*, Hollis and Carter, 1953, vol II. p259.
5. Wrexham Diocesan Archives, John Hugh Jones MS, 19th century.
6. Stonyhurst Anglia, IV, n71, p3, quoted in THOMAS, D. A., *Welsh Elizabethan Catholic Martyrs*, UWP, 1971, p45.
7. CLEARY, J. M., *A checklist of Welsh students in the seminaries*, Pt I, 1568–1603, Cardiff Newman Circle, 1958.
8. CRS, *Miscellanea*, VIII, v13, 1913, p109.
9. CLEARY, J. M., 'Dr Morys Clynnog's invasion projects, 1575–76', in *Recusant History*, v 8, N° 6, 1966.
10. CRS, 22, p96.
11. APC, vol xi, p48.
12. THOMAS, D. A., *The Welsh Elizabethan Catholic martyrs*, UWP, 1971, p21.
13. APC, vol xi, p29
14. APC, vol xiii, pp427–8.
15. THOMAS, D. A., *The Welsh Elizabethan Catholic martyrs*,UWP, 1971, p44.
16. HUGHES, Philip, *The Reformation in England*, vol. 3, p313.
17. PRO, Wales 4 6/1.
18. PRO, Wales 4, 6/7.
19. Holywell, MS.
20. Holywell, MS.
21. NLW Wales, 4, 6/1.
22. Holywell, MS.
23. Holywell, MS.
24. Holywell, MS.
25. NLW Wales, 4, 6/6.
26. Holywell MS.
27. Holywell MS.
28. Holywell MS. The author was probably Fr John Bennett.
29. see JONES, E. G., ' The Lleyn recusancy case 1578–81', *Trans Cymm*, 1936, for figures.
30. APC, xxii, p543.
31. APC, xxii, p544.
32. ELLIS, T. P., *The Catholic martyrs of Wales*, London, 1933, p184.
33. CLEARY, J. M., *A checklist of Welsh students in the seminaries*, Pt 1, 1568–1603, Cardiff, Newman Circle, 1958.
34 CRS, vol 10, 1913, Douai College diaries.
35 CRS, vol 18, *Recusant Roll*, No 1 (1592–3).
36 Records of the Court of Great Sessions, Wales, 4/12/3.
37 CLEARY, J. M., *A checklist of Welsh students in the seminaries*, Pt 1, 1568–1603, Cardiff Newman Circle, 1958.
38. MAGEE, Brian, *The English Recusants: Burns, Oates and Washbourne*, 1938, p83.

CHAPTER TWO

The Seventeenth Century

In many ways the seventeenth century was to become an even harsher time for Catholic recusants. Catholics in the Wrexham area, as elsewhere, would have been affected by the intensification of the penal laws as reign followed reign. Nevertheless, records reveal that, despite such conditions, there was a significant increase in the numbers of recusants in north Wales during the period. Especially in the area of Holywell, there were to be many conversions to Catholicism.

The lives of most Catholics in Wrexham during penal times have disappeared without trace. Because being discovered to be a Catholic, attending Mass or even owning religious objects, could meet with a fine, imprisonment or worse, naturally Catholics led very secret lives and usually left no records. It is generally only when they fell foul of the law, that any evidence is available. Anglican bishops regularly instructed churchwardens to seek out 'popish recusants' in their parishes and notify them of their numbers. When the churchwardens were diligent, we have some idea of the number of Catholics in a particular diocese. The diocesan return of 1603, described later, is a case in point. When people were fined or imprisoned, we have their names, so we can identify some of those who were Catholic recusants in Wrexham or any other place at a particular time. Of course, the names of those who were never discovered did not appear on any documents. So, records of recusant Catholics in Wrexham are few and far between, but nevertheless they give some indication of those who adhered to the faith through very difficult times and they deserve to be remembered.

Toleration rather than restoration of the Catholic faith was what Catholics looked forward to under James I. Their hopes were high, for he was the son of Mary, Queen of Scots, and had promised toleration to Catholics. He had even married a Catholic. Yet, despite his Catholic mother, he had been brought up by Scottish Presbyterians and was to prove a great disappointment to Catholics, who continued to be presented in the courts for their recusancy. In fact, immediately following his accession there was a significant increase in the numbers of those presented in north Wales. Perhaps they had been expecting a relaxation of the penal laws? Despite the numerous hardships heaped upon them, the number of recusants convicted during James I's reign exceeded those convicted between 1581 and 1603.[1]

In Denbighshire, in the hundred of Bromfield, the number of recusants convicted during the period 1581–1624 was 135. Of these, about eighty-six were from the parish of Wrexham. A few were members of the gentry, while the rest were made up of the yeoman class.[2]

The earliest seventeenth-century document which gives us any information regarding recusants in north Wales is the Diocesan Return of 1603, entitled 'A brief sum of all the

Parishes, Impropriations, Preachers, Communicants and Recusants certified for the several dioceses.' Although this gives no names, it lists the numbers of recusants diocese by diocese and so we find that in St Asaph diocese, in which Wrexham lay, there were a total of 250 recusants, 100 men and 150 women. We do not know whether any of them were from Wrexham.[3]

The next record we have, however, tells us a little more about Wrexham. This informs us that a Court of Great Sessions was held on 25 May 1605. At this, Richard Parry, Bishop of St Asaph, presented over 150 recusants for being absent from an Anglican place of worship. Thirty of these were from Wrexham, a mixture of Catholics and Puritans, no doubt.[4]

Later the same year, a small band of fanatical Catholics, frustrated at their position, hatched a plot to blow up King and Parliament. To go down in history as the Gunpowder Plot, this no doubt, fuelled the existing fear of Catholics which was to be so prevalent during the rest of the seventeenth century. Denounced at the time by the whole Catholic body, it resulted in the deaths of two priests and was to be the excuse for even more bitter persecution and further legislation against Catholics. Some of the plotters fled to Wales, hoping to make a last stand there, but found no support among the Welsh.

A Catholic recusant could be fined large sums of money for not attending services at the Anglican Church. In 1592, Edward Puleston of Hafod-y-Wern was fined £100 for absenting himself for five lunar months.[5] Also, Catholic recusants were no longer allowed to carry arms and were banished from London and ten miles around it. So there was no way that a Catholic could attend Parliament or exercise many of the professions. A forfeit was now charged to anyone sending a boy to a continental seminary, while the boy lost the right to his inheritance. Nevertheless, a letter from the Bishop of London to Cecil, James I's Secretary of State, in April 1602, gives some evidence of Welsh students abroad and a strongly recusant Wales at home — 'In the College beyond the seas there be many Welshmen who hold Wales to be almost all recusants.'[6] Surely a case of wishful thinking on their part!

At any rate, at the Court of Great Sessions held in October 1609, the Bishop of St Asaph presented nearly 150 people for recusancy. Twenty-four of these were from Wrexham and district as follows:

Mary, wife of John Goulborne of Esclusham
Elizabeth Dod
Alice, wife of Hugh Yeardley (gent)
Ellis Griffith (smith)
Ralph ap Ellis
Gwen, his wife
Jeffrey ap Ellis
Edmund Griffith
Margaret, his wife
Jane *verch* Hugh ap John Edwards
Thomas ap John Griffiths (yeoman)
William Powell (tailor)
Margaret, his wife
John ap John Hugh (labourer)
Cicely, wife of Griffith ap Griffith (yeoman)
Richard Bannister (gent)

St Winefride's Well at Holywell, a significant place of Catholic pilgrimage throughout history, even during the years of persecution. The rebuilding of the Well House was funded by Lady Margaret Beaufort (the mother of King Henry VII) who was almost certainly also responsible for the rebuilding of the Parish Church at Wrexham at the turn of the sixteenth century. [W. Alister Williams Collection]

Winifred, his wife
Elizabeth Bostock
Robert Clemon (yeoman)
Robert Norris (yeoman)
Cicely, wife of John ap Richard (slater)

In addition, there there were twenty from Chirk (where the Edwards family was still a powerful influence for the 'Old Faith') and thirteen from Llangollen.[7]

The pressure to conform was very strong and very attractive — complete security, the freedom to acquire wealth and pursue a chosen career, as well as providing a good education for any sons. Yet, despite everything, few Denbighshire recusants seem to have conformed, neither is there any evidence for the weakening of their faith by the end of James's reign.

Charles I succeeded to the throne in 1625, by which time Parliament was strongly Puritan. In 1628, it petitioned the king for a renewal of persecution against Catholics. In their 'Petition of Right', Parliament declared illegal many of the king's actions and for taking many steps without the consent of Parliament. They also attacked what they saw as 'innovations' in religion, which were an attempt by the Bishop of London, William Laud, to bring greater reverence into the Anglican services.

Catholic recusants for their part were still trying to practice their religion as well as they could in increasingly difficult circumstances. From the time of the Reformation, there had always been a strong Catholic presence in Holywell in Flintshire, where the shrine of St Winefride continued to be a place of pilgrimage. On the feast of St Winefride, Mass was often celebrated there in the middle of the night, when as many as one hundred Catholics might attend. The authorities knew about it, sending their spies to report the names of those attending. In 1625, the Bishop of Bangor informed the House of Lords , 'There is a great concourse of people to St Winefred's Well in an old chapel near, a public Mass is said continually'[8]

An extraordinary event occurred on St Winefride's Day (3 November) 1629. A huge number of Catholic pilgrims made their way to Holywell 'divers knights, ladies and gentlemen and gentlewomen… to the number of 1500 … and in the general estimation … about 150 priests.' A list gives the names of those present. It is not too fanciful to imagine that there were people there from the Wrexham area.[9]

From 1629–40, King Charles ruled the country without Parliament and as far as religious matters were concerned, was strongly influenced by William Laud, Archbishop of Canterbury. During this time, the lot of Catholics improved and there were no executions. There is evidence that Catholicism was on the increase in the St Asaph diocese. Its bishop wrote to the Archbishop of Canterbury in 1633 that 'the number and boldness of Romish recusants increased much in many places'.[10]

But, when the Long Parliament met in 1641, times became more difficult as the Puritans gained the ascendancy. This must have had an effect on the Catholics of Wrexham. During the Civil War, twenty-two Catholics in north Wales were forced to forfeit two-thirds of their lands to Parliament. Four of these were from Denbighshire. Magdalen Edwards, widow of John Edwards of Plas Newydd, Chirk, was prominent among them.[11]

Charles I's policies and an increasingly Puritan Parliament could not co-exist indefinitely and in 1642, it was to bring about civil war. Catholic recusants were generally on the side of the King and in Wales, many of the gentry were royalist.

When he visited Wrexham in 1642, the King was given an enthusiastic welcome. The following year Wrexham was briefly occupied by Parliamentarians and by 1648, Denbighshire gentry were declaring their loyalty to Parliament. After Charles I's execution, Cromwell became Lord Protector of the Commonwealth.

Meanwhile, the Puritan cause was growing in Wrexham. In 1635, Walter Cradock, who had been suspended by his bishop for 'schismatic' sermons in Cardiff, had been invited to a curacy in Wrexham. Here, he was to attract large crowds to hear him preach as early as six in the morning. It was Cradock, who, according to tradition, converted Morgan Llwyd and he in turn, was to convert many to Puritanism. Cradock remained in Wrexham for only one year, having, it is said, upset the maltsters by emptying the alehouses in the town. To Puritans like Cradock and Llwyd, the Protestant Reformation, as embodied in the Anglican Church, still retained too many relics of Catholicism in its worship and organisation. They and their co-religionists believed in the sole authority of the Bible in matters of church government no less than in doctrinal matters. Morgan Llwyd was passionate about this, becoming a tremendous force in the Wrexham area and is credited, through his preaching, with establishing Non-Conformity in north Wales. By the mid-1650s, under his influence, Wrexham was becoming more and more Puritan, and a place which Catholics would have found less and less comfortable.

In 1655, the Puritans of Wrexham took up arms against a Royalist uprising. But the Puritanism of Wrexham was exceptional. By 1660, there was a widespread desire to restore the monarchy and Sir Thomas Myddleton, a former Republican, proclaimed Charles II as King at Wrexham. Throughout Wales, there was great joy at the restoration of the monarchy and, having had its brief day of glory, Puritan rule was at an end.

Some believe that under Cromwell, there were few Catholic recusants left in Wales.[12] Certainly, by now, the percentage was very small. Others, suggest that Catholicism was experiencing silent growth rather than disappearance.[13] As far as Wrexham is concerned, there is no evidence to show that there were any Catholics in the town in the 1650s.

Catholics welcomed Charles II to the throne as he was known to have some sympathy with Catholicism and had a Catholic wife. During the early part of his reign, although the penal legislation remained in force, no one suffered death on account of religion. Yet people were still being presented at court for not attending services at the Established Church. In the Court of Great Sessions held on 21 September 1660, over fifty people from Wrexham were presented.[14] We do not know whether they were Catholics, Puritans or Quakers for the latter were, by this date, on the increase.

When Edward Hyde, the Lord Chancellor, set about strengthening the State Church by a series of measures to be known as the Clarendon Code, former incumbents, ejected by the Puritans, were now reinstated and in Wrexham, Rowland Owen was restored as vicar, while the church wardens set about repairing and improving the Parish Church at their own expense.

The strengthening of Anglicanism meant that both Puritans on one side and Catholics on the other were brought before the courts in greater numbers. On 17 August 1663, fourteen people from Wrexham were presented by the Grand Jury specifically as Quakers, while thirty-eight were presented as 'Popish recusants'.[15]

Heading this list was Thomas Trevor of Upper Esclus. Described as a gentleman, he was accused as being 'constantly absent' from church. Nevertheless, all of his children had been baptised in the parish church. His sons, Matthew and Robert, were both to marry into

Protestant families and one of Robert's children was baptised in the parish church.

Others on the list were Eustace, Edward and Sylvanus Crue (or Crew). Eustace was an apothecary, having a house and shop in High Street. He had settled in Wrexham by 1649 and died in 1705. Edward also had a shop in the High Street. Described as a gentleman, he was buried in the churchyard on 21 November 1693. Sylvanus, the third brother, was a well-known goldsmith and engraver. Thomas Bostock, described as an 'innkeeper', lived in High Street, at the The Red Lion, the most important inn in the town. In 1670, it contained fourteen hearths, more than any other house except Bryn-y-Ffynnon. Thomas Bostock may therefore have been a man of some substance. Possibly, as in the inns in Holywell, the Star and the Cross Keys, it was a place where Mass could be celebrated for the Catholics in the area without attracting too much attention from the authorities.

He evidently passed on the faith to his son for a George Bostock, probably the son of Thomas and his wife, Ann, was to become a Catholic priest. Born in 1664, he was received into the College at Rome by Fr. William Morgan, the Rector, by order of Cardinal Howard, the Protector. He was ordained on 12 June 1688 in the Church of St John Lateran.[16] He departed for the mission in England on 1 July 1690. He seems not to have returned to Wales, but worked in North Staffordshire or Derbyshire and died on 17 September 1728.[17]

Other Catholics presented before the Grand Jury in 1663 were John Prince (a barber) and James Owens (a mason).

Two years later, in 1665, Bishop George Griffith of St Asaph reported that there were three Catholic physicians in his diocese, one of whom was Dr John Mostyn, who had his headquarters at Wrexham. A member of the Mostyn family of Talacre, an old Catholic family, he had studied for the priesthood at St Omer in France and then at the English College in Rome, which he left in 1653 to study medicine at Padua. He undoubtedly helped to keep the small Catholic flock at Wrexham together.[18]

In 1670, the north Wales district of the Jesuit Mission was formed into what was to be known as the Residence of St Winefride. It was headed by Fr. Humphrey Evans, SJ, a native of Caernarfonshire, who served the Welsh mission for fifty years. Its headquarters were at Holywell and the Catholics at Wrexham would have come under his care.

By this time, there was a strong group in Parliament determined to stamp out Catholicism. The Lord Chief Justice was instructed to issue warrants to search for and apprehend all priests and Jesuits, and remedies were to be provided 'to prevent the growth of popery', but worse was to follow.

On 27 September 1678, a man called Titus Oates presented to the Privy Council his notorious 'Narrative'of an alleged plot, supposedly by a group of Catholics, to murder Charles II. He demanded that everyone he accused should be arrested. He was hailed as 'Saviour of the nation', and his accusations brought about widespread frenzy throughout the country. These were false allegations, but nevertheless, they were taken seriously. The country was swept off its feet and between 1678 and 1681 numerous Catholics died as a result. Priests, against whom no semblance of a charge regarding the so-called plot could be proved, were tried and convicted solely on the grounds of being priests. Towards the end of 1678, pursuivants were sent down to Wales to seek out and arrest priests, but this affected south Wales far more than north Wales.

Fr. John Plessington, who served the Holywell secular misson, must surely have been known to any Catholics in the Wrexham area. Early in 1679, while on a visit to a Mr Massey of Puddington, Cheshire, he was arrested and taken to Chester to be tried on the charge of being a priest. After being dragged on a hurdle through the streets of Chester, he met his end at Gallows Hill, Boughton, Chester on 19 July 1679, by the usual method of hanging, drawing and quartering.[19]

The number who were executed or died in prison as a result of the terror of the Oates Plot may never be known, but it is said that the repercussions in Wales were especially intense and savage on account of the expansion of the Catholic body as a result of conversions. In 1672, there had been thirty-five conversions based on the Jesuit mission at Holywell, while the following year there were over fifty. In 1685, James II (1633–1701), Duke of York, succeeded Charles II. As he had been converted to Catholicism some years earlier, Catholics saw his ascent to the throne as a ray of hope. In 1686, he visited north Wales with his wife, Queen Mary of Modena, making a pilgrimage to Holywell to pray for a son.

However, the accession of a Catholic king had been looked upon with foreboding by Anglicans and Puritans alike. Soon, their worst fears were realised, when he tried to reverse the events of the previous Protestant years. He began by appointing Catholics to positions of influence. He was in a delicate position, but his character could not match the problems he faced, especially in the religious sphere. He issued a proclamation, the Declaration of Indulgence, in 1687 suspending the execution of all penal laws for religious offences and forbidding the imposition of religious oaths as a test for qualifications. This protected Nonconformists and Catholics alike. However, because of the way he attempted to force the Catholic faith on the nation, within four years of his accession, he had hopelessly estranged the State Church and alienated the foremost supporters of the Crown, the Whig party. Furthermore the worst fears of those seeing a link between Catholicism and absolutist rule seemed to be confirmed by James' standing army.

The birth of his son, who would succeed as a Catholic sovereign, weighted the scale even more heavily against James. So the Whigs looked to Holland, where Mary, the wife of William of Orange, was the next in line to the English throne, after James's son. William himself was a grandson of Charles I. Both he and Mary were Protestants. In 1688, William invaded England with Dutch soldiers and James knew that his brief reign was at an end and fled.

For Catholics, one thing which James II had done, which was to have a lasting effect, was the setting up of a more regular system of church government for Catholics for the first time since the Reformation. Four areas of the country, Northern, Western, Midlands and London were each given a bishop in charge, known as a Vicar Apostolic, as they were not ordinary diocesan bishops.

Wales became part of the Western District, which also included the West Country as far as Wiltshire. Dom Michael Ellis, OSB, a Benedictine monk, was the first Vicar Apostolic of the Western District. He was consecrated bishop at St James's Palace on 6 May 1688. On account of the revolution in that year, he was prevented from taking up his position and was eventually to resign in 1705.[20]

At the time of his consecration, he and his three fellow bishops issued a joint pastoral letter to all the faithful. No doubt, they thought that the days of persecution were over. Catholics were able to come out into the open. Clergy could publicly fulfil their religious duties and the new Catholic bishops had been publicly consecrated.

But, hardly had the pastoral letter been issued, when the 'Glorious Revolution' broke out and William and Mary became King and Queen. This was seen as a vindication of the Protestant cause and within a year further laws were enacted against their Roman Catholic subjects.

The heirs of Morgan Llwyd remained an important element in the religious and political life of the town, but some of the Catholics who were in Wrexham in 1663 were still hanging on, while others had joined them. On 17 April 1694, at the Quarter Sessions held in Ruthin, the following were presented by the two High Constables 'ffor popish recusancy', Robert Trevor of Eclustra (i.e. Esclusham), gent. He was the son of the Thomas Trevor presented in 1663. Others were Henry Roberts of Stansty, gent, James Gooden (or Goodwin) of Wrexham, described as a practitioner in physic and Andrew Hill, a cooper. Was this the same Andrew Hill of Pen-y-bryn, Wrexham Abbot, whose wife, Jane died on 23 October 1694?

Eustace Crew, apothecary, appears again, along with Thomas Crue of Holt, possibly a relative. John Mercer, body (bodice) maker may have been the bodice-maker living in The Greene, whose daughter, Anne had been baptised in the Parish Church in 1688. Thomas Bostock, the innkeeper also appeared. He was either the same Thomas Bostock listed in 1663, or he may have been his son. Edward Roberts of Erlas was also presented. His wife was Frances Roberts, 'of Erlas in Gresford parish', who was buried on 26 August 1696.[21]

So the Catholics continued to be ground down. By the last years of the century, a £100 reward was offered to anyone apprehending a popish bishop, priest or Jesuit saying Mass, or exercising any spiritual function. Samuel Pepys, wrote in his diary on 12 April 1700:

> Parliament has proceeded to a greater degree of severity against our Roman Catholics than their predecessors had ever done, by condemning them ... who do not renounce it to take upon them the Protestant religion at or before the age of eighteen, to forfeit their whole inheritance to their next of kin.[22]

And yet, at about this time Celia Fiennes could remark on an 'abundance of the devout papists on their knees around the well' at Holywell, while in that town, the Jesuits and the secular priests continued to baptise and reconcile people to the Catholic Church and minister to the scattered Catholics of north Wales, no doubt including Wrexham, while Bishop Giffard, by now Vicar Apostolic of the Western District, 'travelled through Wales to give confirmation.'[23] It says much for the bravery and tenacity of both bishop and people alike.

References

1. JONES, E. Gwynne, 'Catholic recusancy in the counties of Denbigh, Flint and Montgomery, 1581–1625', *Transactions of the Cymrodorion Society*, 1945, p123.
2. Ibid, p115.
3. Harleian MS 280 pp157–72 quoted in MAGEE, Brian *The English recusants, Burns, Oates and Washbourne*, 1938. p82.
4. NLW Wales 4/13/3.
5. Recusant Rolls 3 and 4, 1594-6, CRS, 61, 1970.
6. Cal SP Domestic 1601–3, p181, Bishop of London to Cecil, 1602 .
7. PRO, Wales 4, 15/2 Certificate of Richard, Bishop of St Asaph.
8. WATKIN, E. I. *Roman Catholicism in England from the Reformation to 1950*, p72 .
9. Quoted in CRS *Miscellanea* III, 1906.
10. Quoted in LEWIS, M. R., 'Wales and the Reformation' in *Yr Hen Ffydd*, No 6, March 2001.
11. KENNEDY, T., 'The Edwards family of Plas Newydd in Chirkland' in *DHST,* vol 41, (1992), pp71–86.
12. WILLIAMS, Llewelyn, *The Making of Modern Wales,* Macmillan, 1919.
13. RICHARDS, Thomas, *Religious Development in Wales (1654–1662),* National Eisteddfod Association, 1923.
14. NLW Wales, 4/25/1.
15. NLW Wales, 4/25/4.
16. CRS *Miscellanea* III, 1906, p108 .

17. KIRK, Rev. John, *Biographies of English Catholics in the 18th Century. Burns, Oates and Washbourne*, 1909.
18. RICHARDS, Thomas, *Religious Developments in Wales (1654–1662)*, National Eisteddfod Association, 1923.
19. ELLIS, T. P., *The Catholic Martyrs of Wales*, London, 1933.
20. BELLENGER, Dom Aidan, *Fathers in Faith*, 1991.
21. PALMER, A. N., *A history of the town of Wrexham*, 2nd ed., 1982.
22. PEPYS, Samuel, *Diary*.
23. WILLIAMS, J. A., *Journal of Ecclesiastical History*, xv, 1964.

CHAPTER THREE

The Eighteenth Century

Material comfort and worldly prosperity were the priorities among the leading classes of British society during the eighteenth century. Indifference to religion of any kind was characteristic of most of the century. In the Anglican Church, there was a marked lack of zeal, with some vicars not even residing in their parishes, as in the case of Wrexham's Dean Shipley, who became Vicar of Wrexham in 1770. Any personal relationship with God was not encouraged generally by the religious Establishment. However, a conversion experience of Howell Harries in south Wales in 1735 was in time to change the religious face of Wales and towards the end of the century, would begin to influence Wrexham.

Many believe that the Catholic Church in Britain reached its lowest ebb during the eighteenth century. For any Catholics in Wrexham, their cause must have seemed hopeless. Yet it was during that period that seeds would be sown, which would contribute to the eventual revival of Catholicism in the nineteenth century.

The 1700 Act of Succession meant that, subsequently, Catholics were to be excluded from the English throne, while in 1697, the House of Commons had petitioned the king for the removal of papists and non-jurors from London.[1] Many of the very rich in contact with the Court were among the first to abandon the Catholic faith, while among the gentry, there was a steady, very gradual decline.[2]

However, there is evidence that there was still a group of Catholics in Wrexham by the opening of the eighteenth century. There were fifteen of them altogether, compared with seven in 1663 and nine in 1694. Some of them were the same as those listed in both 1663 and 1694 or members of their families. A document still in existence records the names of 'popish recusants within the parish of Wrexham' at that time as follows:

Mr Matthew Trevor and Elizabeth, his wife.
Mr Robert Trevor
Edmund Davies, widower
Elizabeth, wife of John ap John
Uxor (wife of) John Thomas Williams
Uxor (wife of) Mr Hugh Meredith
Eustace Crwe
Edward Crwe
Mr James Goodin or Goodwin
Andrew Hill & uxor (wife)
Mrs Rondler, widow
Petronella Crwe
Henry Roberte
Uxor (wife of) Edward Roberte

Matthew Trevor was the son of Thomas Trevor, gent of Esclusham, presented as a recusant in 1663. Robert was probably his other son. Both married into Protestant families. Alternatively, he may have been Robert's son. Eustace Crew, if he is the same as the one listed in 1663, was an apothecary and must have been an old man by now. Mr James Gooden or Goodwin was a practitioner in physic and appeared in the list of recusants in1694. Andrew Hill may have been a cooper of Pen-y-bryn.[3]

There were fears that Catholicism along with Nonconformity was on the increase and in 1702, an act to require a new oath to be made by its adherents came into force. By 1710, an act for the erection of fifty new Anglican churches was made to address the 'inconvenience and growing mischief which result from the increase of Dissenters and Popery'.[4] The following year all Catholic devotions were declared unlawful and the property of Catholics was, in future, to be divided equally between the children. This had the effect of impoverishing the remaining Catholic aristocracy, and in turn, affecting those Catholics dependent upon them.

Yet it was at about this time, in 1713, that a most significant event for the future of Catholicism in Wales was to occur. In that year, a Franciscan bishop, Matthew Prichard was appointed Vicar Apostolic of the Western District, which included Wales. Some believe that it had been for want of a bishop in 1688, that Wales had drifted even further from the Catholic faith.

Many still hankered after the Stuarts as rightful heirs to the throne. These included many Anglicans as well as Catholics and they became known as Jacobites. Following the rebellion in the north in 1715, there was strict punishment of all Catholics who took part in it. It was to become a pretext for the seizure of the land of Catholic gentry, many of whom gave up their faith at this time and conformed to the Anglican Church.

Feelings ran high and this

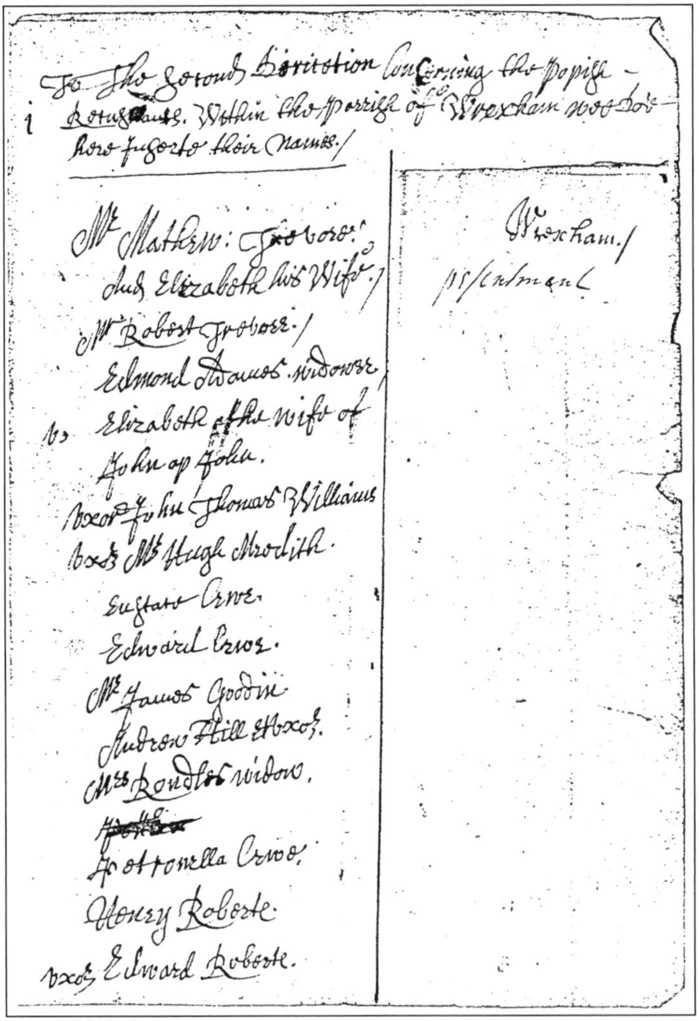
To the Second Direction Concerning the popish Recusants. Within the parrish of Wrexham wee doe here insert their Names./

Mr Matthew: Trevor: and Elizabeth his Wife./ — Wrexham./
Mr Robert Trevor./
Edmond Davies. widower,
Elizabeth the wife of John ap John.
uxor John Thomas Williams
uxor Mr Hugh Meredith.
Eustace Crewe
Edward Crewe.
Mr James Goodin
Andrew Hill et uxor.
Mrs Rondles widow.
Petronella Crewe,
Henry Roberts.
uxor Edward Roberts.

The early eighteenth century presentment of 'Popish Recusants in Wrexham'.
[Denbighshire Record Office, DD/DM/228/4]

impinged on the life of Wrexham, when in 1715 riots broke out in the town, disorder reigning for about a fortnight during which time both of the meeting houses of the Dissenters were wrecked by the mob, who were eventually joined by the colliers of the surrounding districts.[5]

Meanwhile, an Act was passed in the same year requiring Catholics to register their lands. An imposition of a tax, amounting to two-thirds of their value had the force of law. It was rarely executed, but they were obliged to pay a double land tax and to enrol their title deeds. The landed families' survival was crucial to the survival of Catholicism, which centred on their country houses, where Mass might be said by their chaplain, if there was one, or by an itinerant priest, usually being passed off as a manservant.[6]

At the Quarter Sessions held at Ruthin in 1723 under this Act, the following registered their estates, so we know that these Catholics at least, were living in the Wrexham area at the time:

Anne Davies of Wrexham[7]
Jacob Wilson of Wrexham
Mary Middleton of Wrexham
Thomas Lloyd, Minera, Chirk, Wrexham
Elizabeth Lloyd, Wrexham
Dorothy Puleston, Gresford, Wrexham[8]

Furthermore, a couple of years later, the Bishop of Chester's Returns for Catholics in his diocese, reveal that there were other Catholics living in the area. There were twenty-five around Holt including members of the latest generation of the Crew family.[9]

The authorities continued to be on the alert for the very presence of Catholics. However it appears that at local level, the local officers were failing in their duty. A list, dated 1744, is still extant of 'constables defaulting in submitting lists of papists from the townships and parishes in the hundreds of . . . . . Bromfield and Chirk'.[10]

Bishop Prichard, Vicar Apostolic of the Western District in which Wrexham lay, died in 1750. Bishop Laurence York, a Benedictine, succeeded him. He would have been affected, as would his flock, by the Hardwick Marriage Act of 1753 which declared null and void any marriage in England and Wales which was not celebrated according to the rites of the Established Church. Both Jews and Quakers were exempt from this, but Dissenters, which, under the law included Catholics, were not. The way out of the dilemma for Catholics was to have two ceremonies. Arguments went on among Catholics for several generations as to which ceremony should precede the other. A

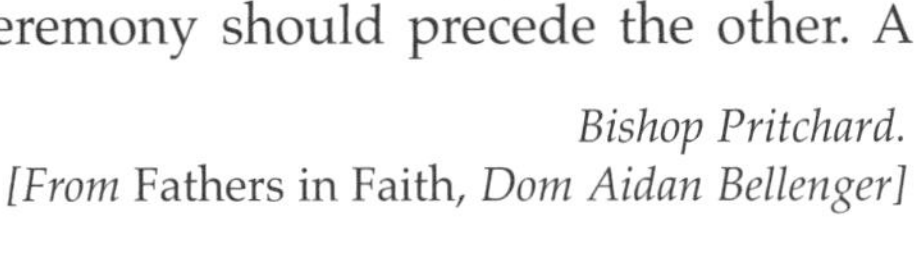

Bishop Pritchard.
[From Fathers in Faith, *Dom Aidan Bellenger]*

priest could expect to be transported if he contravened the law and further source of worry to the clergy, was the temptation for ill-disposed persons to act as informers. Under an act of 1699 a reward of £100 was offered to anyone bringing about the successful prosecution of a priest.

The shrine at Holywell was continuing to attract Catholic pilgrims, who came from all parts of the realm. From there, the priests travelled around north Wales, keeping in touch with their scattered Catholic flock, including those living in the Wrexham area. The parish registers of Holywell confirm this. In a copy of 'Rev. Mr Gwillim's Register' of the Cross Keys, we find the following entries, 'Baptized 1755 July 21 at Wrexham, James the son of a breeches maker and the following year, 1756, September 20th Mary, daughter of Thos Winstanley, a clockmaker at Wrexham'.[11] Rev. John Gwillim had been educated at Lisbon and was to die in Holywell on 3 April 1763.[12]

As a result of scientific discoveries of the previous hundred years, industry began to develop in Britain at a very fast rate. Huge numbers of people began to move from the countryside into areas which were growing into sprawling, insanitary and overcrowded towns. In the Wrexham area, coal and iron and other minerals were being mined much more efficiently than previously. Yet, because of the lack of both capital and good roads, industrial development fell well behind that of England. But, later in the century, as new roads and canals were built, English capitalists were drawn to the area, attracted by the raw materials and cheap labour. At the same time there were also developments in agriculture. 'Improvement' was a word which was in the air.

Wrexham continued to be the main market town in north Wales. Its population, (only to be 2,575 by 1801)[13] saw a vast increase at the time of the Great March Fair. Dr Johnson, visiting the town in the second-half of the eighteenth century found it a 'busy, extensive and well-built town'.[14]

By 1763/4, the Catholics of Wales welcomed Bishop Walmesley, as the new Vicar Apostolic of the Western District. Bath, where he resided, was the principal mission of his district.

There was a handful of Catholics in Wrexham at about this time. A list, dated 21 November 1767, signed by the Bishop of St Asaph, suggests that there were at least seven.[15] Unfortunately, we do not know their names, but there was a farmer aged seventy-three, his older sister and his daughter of twenty-five, a fifty-year-old wife of an attorney, a forty-year-old schoolmaster and his wife and an old lady of eighty who sold gingerbread. We do not know whether they had been born in the town, or whether they had moved in from elsewhere. On the same list there were 176 Catholics in Holywell, and 47 in St

Facing: Wrexham, S & N Buck, 1748.

Right: Bishop Walmesley.
[From Fathers in Faith, *Dom Aidan Bellenger]*

Asaph — some measure of the success of the Jesuit mission at Holywell. Also listed were ten at Nercwys, near Mold, home of the recusant Giffard family. They need to be given the credit for helping to sustain the Catholic communities in the counties of Flintshire and Denbighshire in the eighteenth century and into the early part of the nineteenth century.

In his returns to Rome of 1773, Bishop Walmesley reported of Wales that there were about 750 Catholics, with 9 priests and 7 public chapels. There were no Catholic chapels in north Wales at this date.[16]

The Catholic Relief Act of 1778, at what is now thought to have been at a time of modest gain for Catholicism, came as the first chink of light after a long, dark night of persecution. The Government, wanting to recruit Scottish Catholic highlanders to help in the war against the American colonies, made overtures to the Scottish Bishop Hay to ask what measure of relief for Catholics might make recruitment successful. The result was the repeal of the statute of William III, with its reward to informers, penalty of life-imprisomnent for bishops, priests and schoolmasters and the prohibition on the inheritance or purchase of land. In return, Catholics were expected to take an oath of allegiance, agreed to by Bishop Challoner of the London District. This scant measure was paid for at a price. It stirred up underlying depths of fear among Protestants, especially Dissenters, culminating in the Gordon Riots of 1780. The new Catholic chapel at Bath and the house of Bishop Walmesley, were burned down and all his papers lost in the fire.

Despite this, life was becoming easier for Catholics, although they were still not on the same footing as their Protestant neighbours. In 1791, a bill was presented to Parliament 'to relieve, upon conditions and under restrictions the persons therein described, certain penalties and disabilities to which persons professing the Popish religion are by law subject'.[17] To become known as the Catholic Relief Act, it passed into law later the same year. Many of the previous penal restrictions on Catholics were removed. The celebration of Mass for which a priest had been tried in the courts as late as the 1770s was no longer a punishable offence and Catholic places of worship were no longer illegal, although they were allowed to have neither steeple nor bell.

In the following year, on 12 January 1792, John Giffard of Nercwys took the 'Oath of Allegiance, Abjuration and Declaration' at Flintshire Quarter Sessions. At the same time, he registered his house as 'a place of meeting for religious worship.'[18] Mr John Bew, a Catholic priest, fleeing from the French Revolution, became his chaplain. An able priest, he was appointed the first President of Oscott two years later. It was to Nercwys that Catholics in the Wrexham area would have travelled to Mass until Fr. John Briggs began coming to the Wrexham area from Chester in the 1820s.

By the end of the eighteenth century, as the penal laws were relaxed, the practice of their faith became much easier for the Catholics of Wrexham, along with all parts of the kingdom. The late eighteenth century saw modest growth in the Catholic community in general and may have had a slight impact on the growth of Catholicism in Wrexham. A few Irish settled here by the 1790s, pre-dating the influx due to the Irish famine of the 1840s. Whether they were Catholics practising or not, we shall never know. Although the Catholic Church on the continent was in disarray, the Catholic community here could look to the new century with some optimism.

References

1. MURPHY, *The Catholic Church in England and Wales.*
2. MATJTIEW, David, *Catholicism in England,* 2nd ed., Eyre and Spottiswood, 1948.
3. DD/DM/228/4 and PALMER, *A History of the Town of Wrexham,* 1893.
4. MURPHY, *The Catholic Church in England and Wales.*
5. DODD, A. H., *A History of Wrexham,* 1957.
6. WATKIN, E. I., *Roman Catholicism in England from the Reformation to 1950,* OUP, 1957, p105.
7. DRO, QSD/D4/2/2.
8. DRO, QSD/D4/2/3.
9. *Archaeologia Cambrensis,* 1908, p343.
10. DRO, QSD/DA/2/6.
11. Holywell Registers in CRS III, 1906.
12. KIRK, Rev. John, *Biographies of English Catholics in the 18th Century, Burns Oates and Washbourne,* 1909.
13. WILLIAMS, W. Alister, *The Encyclopaedia of Wrexham,* Bridge Books, 2001.
14. DODD, A. H., *A History of Wrexham,* 1957, p84.
15. Diocese of Chester Return of Papists 1767, CRS, 0cc Pubs No 1, 1980.
16. WHYTE, J. H., 'The Vicars' Apostolic returns of 1773', *Recusant History,* vol 9, 1968.
17. 31 Geo III, c32.
18. FRO Quarter Sessions, 12 January 1792.

CHAPTER FOUR

The Nineteenth Century

Britain was to see far-reaching changes and unprecedented growth during the nineteenth century. The changes in society, especially the development of industry, had a significant impact on the religious life of the nation. Attracted by its wealth of ironstone and coal, now made more accessible by improved roads together with the prospect of cheap labour, many English ironmasters were coming across the border into Wales by the beginning of the century. Among these was John Thompson, a Catholic who, with his family, settled in the Wrexham area about 1813.[1] They had come from Wigan, the head of a great coalmining district, where John and his brother, James, had ironmerchants' businesses in adjoining streets in the town. They continued to keep an interest there and a 'Thompsons Ironmerchants' was still found at 14 Millgate, Wigan, on the eve of the Second World War.

Iron production in the Wrexham area was just coming out of a boom period, when there had been a great demand for cannon and shot on account of the Napoleonic Wars, 1797–1815. A period of decline was to follow but, although there was a slump generally, in the Wrexham area, it was expanding. Coal was by now being used in the iron-smelting process and so ironmasters benefited from having a coalmine adjacent to their ironworkings, which was often the case in the area around Wrexham. John Thompson leased the Ponciau Ironworks in 1813 and he worked the Brymbo Ironworks from 1819 to 1829. He also opened Ffrwd Furnace in 1824, keeping it in full blast till 1842. It was said that the 'one time peaceful Vale of Maelor was now awakened by the incessant din of industrial operations. Parishes like Ruabon had their hillsides tunnelled with pits and levels, whilst the ironworks belched forth thick clouds of smoke to darken the district.'[2]

Hand in hand with the flourishing iron industry went the development of agriculture in the adjoining districts. John Thompson was involved with this too, always ready to try out new methods. These industries had the effect of attracting many people from rural to industrial areas, so that between 1800 and the 1850s the population of Wrexham and Ruabon more than doubled.

Locally, John Thompson came to be seen as a very successful ironmaster. A letter in the *Chester Courant* of 9 February 1827 stated that 'he was perhaps one of the most extensive ironmasters throughout the United Kingdom.' A letter a fortnight later pointed out that, successful as he had been, perhaps making 100 tons of iron a month, this could not compare with ironmasters in south Wales, who were able to make 3,000 tons. Nevertheless, he did well and laid the foundations of his fortunes, to be built up further by his son, Richard. In turn, this was to enable Richard to be a great benefactor to the Catholics in the town, through both St David's Chapel, King Street and St Mary's Church, Regent Street.

The Thompson family was deeply attached to the Catholic faith, their birthplace, Wigan,

Father John Briggs
[Leeds Diocesan Archives].

being one of the most Catholic towns in Britain, with 2,000 Catholics living there in 1810.[3] John and James had a younger brother, Richard, who studied for the priesthood at Douai and distinguished himself by hiding some of the college's valuables at the time of the French Revolution. He was ordained priest in 1797 and eventually became Vicar General of the Northern District. John was to name his son after him.

On 18 October 1827, Richard married Helen Bourke at St Werburgh's Catholic Church in Chester. Her family came from Tipperary in Ireland. The priest who married them was Fr. John Briggs, who had been serving at Chester since 1816 and had already explored the Wrexham area in search of Catholics. Later, he was to become Bishop of Beverley.

For the Catholic community nationally, the early decades of the nineteenth century were marked by the struggle for religious emancipation. This was to be met with resistance and became a most persistent political problem in early nineteenth century Britain. King George III was deeply opposed to it and his opposition was reflected in north Wales. A petition was sent from Denbigh in 1807 urging Parliament to adhere firmly to the Protestant interest.[4]

The supporters of Catholic Emancipation looked to the new King, George IV, to further their cause, but the Catholic Emancipation Bills of 1821 and 1825 were both defeated. Wrexham Parish Vestry Minutes of 20 April 1825 reveal the concerns of some of the leading citizens of Wrexham, should the Bill of 1825 become law. A petition was unanimously agreed to by the ministers, churchwardens and other parishioners and sent to both houses of Parliament 'against any further concessions to Roman Catholics … they were truly anxious that they should enjoy religious toleration … but we cannot view the admission of Roman Catholics into offices of political trust and power without sensations of intense anxiety and alarm for the safety of our excellent Protestant Establishment … .'

The signatories of the petition were:

Ebenezer Williams, curate
D. Hughes, curate
George Kenyon, 2nd baron Gredington (1776–1855), educated at Harrow and Oxford, barrister.
R. M. Lloyd, a leading member of Wrexham society in the early eighteenth century. Son of Richard Lloyd, founder of Lloyd's bank, High Sheriff of Denbighshire, JP, and Vicar's Warden at the Parish Church.
Richard Lewis
John Hutchison
Bartholomew Dillon, in turn a prosperous wine merchant, schoolmaster, successful accountant, who went bankrupt in 1842.
William Gummow, most likely a member of the Gummow family of architects and builders
Thomas Broster[5]

The Bill was heavily defeated in the House of Lords.

Wrexham was not the only place where people were strongly against further concessions to Catholics. By now, Calvinistic Methodism had greatly increased, so that north Wales had become something of a Protestant stronghold and in some places fiercely anti-Catholic.

Bishop Collingridge, the Vicar Apostolic of the Western District, which included Wrexham, saw it his duty:

> to watch over and promote … the interest of religion in this extensive district … in which, for want of temporal means, the Catholic religion is scarcely known in many parts, particularly in … all Wales, North and South.'[6]

His episcopate was a most fruitful one for Wales. Known as a learned and saintly bishop, he did what he could to address the needs of his district. He is known to have visited north Wales in 1810 and 1813, when he confirmed several people at the Star, Holywell, where he came 'in the time of the Rev'd Edward Wright'and where Wrexham Catholics would have had to travel for the sacrament of confirmation.[7]

At the beginning of the nineteenth century, Catholics in Wrexham still occasionally attended Mass, in a private chapel attached to Nerquis Hall through the zeal of Miss Mary Eleanor Giffard, who died September 16th, 1808 … After Miss Giffard's death Holy Mass was continued to be said in the same private chapel until the death of her Protestant sister, Elizabeth Giffard, which occurred on 19th March, 1842. For two years afterwards Mass was occasionally said in a farmhouse about a mile from the Hall by the priest attached to the Mission of Wrexham.[8] Mass had been celebrated at Nerquis Hall since at least 1792.[8]

When John Thompson settled at Brymbo about 1813, Mass was also celebrated at his home from time to time. Then probably, by about 1820, Fr. John Briggs came from Chester to Wrexham on weekdays and

> … the first Mass [there] was in Market Street next to the Beast Market. The woman who let the room for the priest did not like it and so he had to find another room nearby. At this time, a Catholic hardly dare show himself.[9]
>
> Tis said that a man ventured into the room of Mass and standing in the middle exclaimed 'What a sacrifice!' Waiting quietly until the elevation was over (it had begun) , Jack and Thom Flanagan went to him, seized him by the collar and taking him out, pitched him into the middle of the road and he and a small crowd went away quietly and ever after there was no disturbance in a Catholic meeting.[10]

Meanwhile, Fr. John Briggs was busily looking out for Catholics in the area. Writing on 7 April 1824 to Bishop Collingridge, he said:

I was at Wrexham yesterday and found about thirty

Bishop Peter Bernardine Collingridge.
[From Fathers in Faith, *Dom Aidan Bellenger]*

Catholics in the town. I believe there may be nearly twenty more in the country about Wrexham ... I have also to submit to your Lordship's approbation my design of taking a larger and respectable room in Wrexham and during the summer months giving public instructions to the Catholics and any Protestants that may attend.[11]

The 'larger and respectable room' may have been the one in Cutler's Entry, Charles Street, where Mass was celebrated until the building of the chapel in King Street. In June of the same year, Fr. Briggs again wrote to the Bishop, this time asking for an assistant, as 'so extensive is the country around Chester (where he lived) both in north Wales and Cheshire, that I am unable to give anything like sufficient attention to the many Catholics scattered almost in every part of this large tract of country'.[12] But it appears that the Bishop was unable to supply him with an assistant.

By 1827, there were enough Catholics in the area for Fr. Briggs to think about the building of a chapel. Writing to Bishop Collingridge from Chester on 4 December he said:

. . . we are making every exertion to raise a chapel at Wrexham . . . where my flock amounts to sixty or seventy and where there is a flattering prospect of forming soon a large and useful Mission. It will, I trust, diffuse its blessings to the neighbouring towns and villages where there are several Catholics scattered without any Pastor to watch over them or assist them in their dying moments.'[13]

He asks the bishop to recommend the venture to the Catholic public, from whom, no doubt, he hoped for donations. He went on to say, 'My principal resource is among the Catholics of the Northern District; my flock at Wrexham being all poor with one exception.[14]

St David's Chapel, King Street

Fr. John Briggs' desire for a chapel was realised on 4 July 1828, when St David's Chapel was opened in King Street.

Wrexham seems to have been expanding and the building of King Street in what were then open fields is some indication of this. The previous year had seen the lighting of Wrexham's streets for the first time and by now Wrexham could boast sixty dealers in foodstuffs and drugs and thirty-two in clothing. Yet, there was a dark side. The working classes in Wrexham 'lived for the most part in wretched hovels or else in sewerless unhealthy closes of which so many existed [there] ... Typhoid and smallpox were endemic.'[15] Most of the Catholics for whom the chapel was built, would have been familiar with these conditions, as they were nearly all very poor.

The land for the chapel had been purchased by Richard Thompson, by now twenty-nine years-of-age. The story goes that the vendor 'finding that a Catholic chapel was to be built thereon, contended against the sale as he had sold the land for a house. A lawyer advised to build a priest's house on the ground and then they could build what they liked upon it and so it was done, the chapel being over the house' [as can be seen today]. When the Protestants etc heard that a Catholic chapel was to be built, they said they would pull it down. Mr Thompson [said] 'I'll set up a blast furnace and send the smoke into the Town Hall. Sir Watkyn [Williams Wynn] is said also to have taken our part.'[16]

Described as a 'neat and commodious edifice ... with a convenient dwelling for the clergyman attached. It was erected by subscription, under the auspices of Richard Thompson Esq of Brymbo, with the co-operation of Protestants.'[17] Donations doubtless

Stansty Hall, the home of the Thompson family. [W. Alister Williams Collection]

included those from the Catholic heartland of Lancashire, where the Thompson family still had connections.

The *Shrewsbury Chronicle* went on to describe the High Mass at the opening of the chapel (the first in north Wales since the Reformation) as 'imposing', while Mozart's setting of the Mass provided a 'rich treat' for lovers of sacred music. The nuns of Shepton Mallet had provided the vestments and altar requisites for the new chapel.[18] The event 'brought together a considerable number of the gentry and respectable inhabitants of Wrexham and district.' Roman Catholics came from as far as Liverpool and Chester and the chapel was full, despite admission being 4/- and 2/-. Bishop Penswick, the co-adjutor Vicar Apostolic of the Northern District, was the chief celebrant, assisted by Rev. J. Hall of Macclesfield, Rev. J. Fisher of Stone, Rev. J. Briggs of Chester, Rev. William Collingridge of Hooton and a dozen other clergy. The choir came from Copperas Chapel, Liverpool and Rev. Francis Martyn, who worked for twenty-four years as a missioner in the Black Country with outstanding success, preached eloquently. One wonders how many poor people attended!

Fifty ladies and gentlemen sat down to dinner at 3pm at the Eagles Hotel [now the Wynnstay], John Thompson taking the head of the table. Clearly inter-denominational relations were good at this time in Wrexham, for there were numerous toasts, including that to 'Mr Griffiths (of the Mount) and the Liberal Protestants who have this day honoured us with their presence'. Mr Griffiths, replying to the toast, said he believed in the freedom of religion and liberty of conscience, which he claimed for himself. He hoped the day was not far distant, when his Roman Catholic brethren would be admitted within the pale of the Constitution, by the removal of the remaining disabilities under which they now laboured. He wished the new chapel every possible success and prosperity and he hoped that Catholic/Protestant enmities and prejudices, which had for ages kept them asunder, would gradually disappear. The final toast to 'the cause of civil and religious liberty all over the world', brought much applause. The company departed at 7.30pm, pleased with the day's proceedings.[19]

Mr Griffiths must have been very pleased when the remaining difficulties under which his Roman Catholic brethren in Wrexham laboured were, by and large, removed the following year, 1829, when the Catholic Emancipation Act became law. The struggle for emancipation had been gradual and had been met with resistance at every stage.

The 1829 Act, by which Catholics were put on the same footing as their Protestant neighbours, except for a few restrictions, largely came about because the government, alarmed at growing tensions in Ireland, needed to take measures to placate the Catholics there. It meant that Catholicism was no longer an underground religion and Wrexham's Catholic population must have felt a greater sense of security as they could now display their religion more openly. The next quarter-century saw a period when public opinion generally began to yield to the spirit of toleration. Nevertheless, under the surface, public opinion, especially in north Wales was decidedly opposed to Catholic relief. The *North Wales Chronicle* had asserted in 1828 that the Calvinistic Methodists of Wales were unanimously anti-Catholic. Controversy did not end with the 1829 Act. Later in the century, British public opinion was to show that it was as intolerant of Catholicism as ever.

The loosening of restrictions could not have come at a better time for the Catholic Church which throughout Europe had been in a decaying state at the end of the eighteenth century. But new shoots were sprouting on old roots as Catholicism began to expand in the towns and the religious orders, expelled in the aftermath of the French Revolution, returned to Britain, after a gap of over two hundred years. Meanwhile, Fr. John Briggs, writing to Bishop Collingridge from Chester on 26 June 1828, felt that the

> prospect of doing much good there [in Wrexham] is much brighter than what I had supposed ... When I arrived on Sunday I found that there had been a very numerous and respectable assemblage at the Chapel at the hours of 10 and 12 o'clock ... and the Chapel was crowded at 7 o'clock quite to suffocation. Besides about twenty that have presented themselves for instruction some other Protestants have bespoken sittings in the Chapel.

He goes on to say that it would be utterly impossible to procure a clergyman [for Wrexham] from the Northern District and discusses the financial arrangements for the support of the Mission.[20]

Catholics in Wrexham, desiring the sacrament of confirmation still had to go to Holywell. Thus it was, that Susan Kelly from Wrexham made her way there on 14 November 1833 to be confirmed in the new chapel. It had been opened the previous day by Bishop Briggs at the request of Dr Baines, Vicar Apostolic of the Western District, in whose area Holywell lay at the time. Clearly this would have saved him a very long journey. By now Bishop Briggs was Co-adjutor to Bishop Penswick of the Northern District.[21]

The congregation which gathered at St David's chapel on Sunday mornings would have been very mixed. First of all, there was the Thompson family growing rich through their ventures in coalmining and iron production. John Thompson, by this date was a well-established ironmaster. His son, Richard, was following in his footsteps and by 1832 had built Stansty Hall for himself, his Irish wife, and twin children, John and Mary-Ann. Both father and son were acquiring land and properties in the area roughly between what are now the A525 and A541. Richard interested himself in the town, becoming a Justice of the Peace in the early 1840s.

Then there was Charles Bate and his wife, Eliza. He was a member of a landed family — the Bates of Marchwiel. In 1841, he was described as a bricksetter and innkeeper — landlord of the Union Tavern in Yorke Street. He went on to become a brewer, employing three men by 1851. There was also Simon Wallwork, a grocer, living in High Street. And then there were the Irish. By 1841 (the year of the census), there was a Roman Catholic congregaton of about 280, generally poor.[22]

St David's Chapel, King Street, Wrexham. The above photograph was taken in the 1930s, shortly before the front was removed to make way for shop premises at ground floor level. [W. Alister Williams Collection]

The photograph on the left shows the premises after conversion to shops and living accommodation.

There were over 160 adults living in Wrexham who had been born in Ireland.[23] Some of them would have been Protestants and no doubt many would have been Catholics in name only. It is thought that in Ireland at this time only about 40% of Catholics practised their faith. The Irish did not form a ghetto, as such, but being unskilled by and large, lived in the poorer parts of the town, mainly in Mount Street, Salop Street, Brook Street and the Old Yorkshire Hall. Most of them were described as 'Labourers' (33) or 'hawkers' (29) on the 1841 census, but there were six shoemakers, three coachmen, a weaver and a law student as well as the Catholic priest, Fr. John Tobin or Mr Tobin, as he would have been called at this time.[24]

Most Irish men were married to Irish women, but there was some intermarriage between the Irish, the Welsh and the English. Then there were those who had joined the Catholic Church, since the opening of the chapel, numbering twenty-eight by 1841. These included the family of Meredith Humphreys, a labourer from Broughton, who had been received into the Catholic Church in the 1830s. Such a mixture of backgrounds may have caused some tensions.

The services would have been very plain, the faith of the Welsh and English being very reserved, coming as they were out of a period of persecution. Their personal spirituality would have been inspired by Bishop Challoner's 'Garden of the soul'. The faith of the Irish, on the other hand would have reflected the seasonal rhythms of life, springing out of their Celtic spirituality. This may have seemed to the English and Welsh as bordering on superstition. There would have been very little ornament in the chapel (an inventory of 1841 lists no statues, pictures etc) and devotions, such as that to the Sacred Heart, which we now take for granted, were to spread from the Continent during the next decade along with clerical dress. Until this time, the clergy, seeking a low profile, would normally have worn brown.

In 1841, about forty people were confirmed in the chapel by Bishop Brown, including Mary Ann Thompson.[25] The chapel, which had had the addition of a porch the previous year, was described by Fr. Tobin as:

> badly put together, tho the chapel cost £1,000 upwards. The recent woodwork in the gallery is in a bad state, having not been done in a workmanlike manner. There is a debt on the chapel of £300.[26]

Further reference to this appears in the *Laity's Directory* for 1842, where the destitution of the Vicariate of Wales is described as 'in every way extreme.' In an appeal for funds, the chapel is described as being:

> still encumbered with a debt of £300, even the interest upon which the Rt Rev. Vicar Apostolic of the District has no present means of paying. Neither has the Rev incumbent whose annual income including all the perquisites of his mission amount to no more than £84, unless by subjecting himself to very great privations. The aid of the charitable is therefore most earnestly supplicated'[27]

As well as his duties in Wrexham, at about this time, Fr. Tobin, Wrexham's missioner, took on the further responsibility of celebrating Mass for about 100 Catholics in Mold. By 1847, it is said that there were 300 Roman Catholics in Wrexham, but whether they were all at the chapel on Sunday mornings, we do not know. At any rate, it seems impossible that it could have accommodated even half that number.

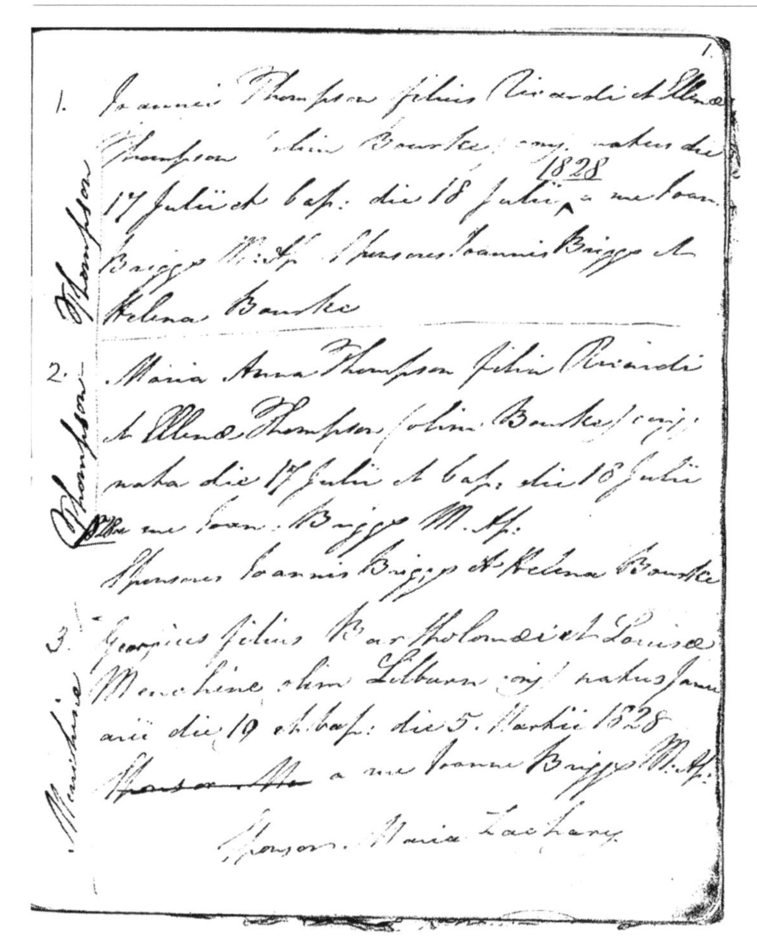

1\.
Thompson
Joannes Thompson filius Ricardi et Ellenæ Thompson olim Bourke, conj. natus die 17 Julii et bap: die 18 Julii 1828 a me Joan. Briggs M. Ap. Sponsores Joannis Briggs et Helena Bourke

2\.
Thompson
Maria Anna Thompson filia Ricardi et Ellenæ Thompson (olim Bourke) conj. nata die 17 Julii et bap. die 18 Julii a me Joan. Briggs M. Ap.
Sponsores Joannis Briggs et Helena Bourke

3\.
Menchine
Georgius filius Bartholomæi et Louisæ Menchine olim Lilburn conj. natus Januarii die 19 et bap: die 5 Martii 1828 a me Joanne Briggs M. Ap.
Sponsor Maria Zachary

The entry for the Thompson twins in the Baptism Register, July 1828. [A. N. Palmer Centre]

For whom was St Mary's built?

The reasons why St Mary's Church was built were many. The most pressing reason was that St David's Chapel had now become too small for the congregation. But who were they? Something about the people for whom it was built can be gleaned by bringing various records together to give us a picture of those who made their way to St Mary's through the streets of Wrexham on a Sunday morning. Meanwhile, Wrexham itself had changed and was changing.

In the *Wrexham Recorder* for 1848, a writer reflected how, during the previous twenty-five years, Wrexham had been converted from a decayed 'genteel town where but lately many of the neighbouring gentry had kept up town houses — into something like an improved and improving commercial one'. The population had grown apace, people crowding into the town as industry developed. There were to be twice as many inhabitants in the Wrexham of 1851 than that of fifty years previously. Of course, Catholics were among their number. As well as the Irish, escaping from the potato famine, there were also those coming over the border from Chester, which had a high Catholic population. Unlike the towns of south Wales, Wrexham did not see a huge influx of Irish. It was more like a steady trickle and it had begun back in the 1790s, well before the famine. From a religious point of view, Wrexham could be described more as a Nonconformist town by mid-century. By now, apart from St Giles, the Anglican church and St David's Roman Catholic chapel, there were nine Nonconformist chapels of various denominations and sizes.

The census, taken every ten years, was taken in 1851. For the first time, there was also a religious census which gives us a picture of where Wrexham people attended church or chapel and how many of them did so.

Attendance on Census Sunday in the various places of worship was as follows:

	Morning	*Afternoon*	*Evening*
St Giles	1,000	60 [Welsh service]	600
St David's R C Chapel	240	40	80
Nonconformists	928	631	1,129

A criticism made against the figures in the Religious Census is that they are confusing, as we do not know whether those attending their place of worship in the afternoon or evening are some of the same people attending in the morning or not. In the case of Catholics, afternoon or evening attendance would be additional. Then, as now, the Mass was the main service. It is not until relatively recently that it has been allowed to celebrate it at any other time but the morning. The figure of 240 therefore represents those attending Mass in the morning, some of them returning for an additional service. Just how 240 people could have fitted into the Catholic chapel, even with its 1840 extension, cannot be imagined. The number, anyway, is misleading. The census day fell on Sunday, 30 March at the time of the March Fair, attended by many people from far and wide. Among their number were strolling players, musicians, hawkers and pedlars, many from Ireland.

The names of 711 Irish-born people, both residents and visitors appear on the general census, so if they were all Catholic, and some would have been Protestant, only about a third of the Irish Catholic population of Wrexham on census day would have attended Mass in addition to those who were not Irish.

However, the majority of the regular congregation attending St David's Chapel on a Sunday continued to be from Ireland. By 1851, they had increased in number, arriving in Wrexham via Chester, Manchester and other English towns. In about half of the Catholic families in Wrexham, both parents were Irish. For the rest, lines were becoming blurred by inter-marriage with the Welsh and English. Families were generally not as large as sometimes supposed. Of 332 of these families found in Wrexham between 1828 and 1851, 233 had only one child, 53 families had two children and 25 families had three children. Nevertheless, there were a few large families such as the Mulligans who had twelve children.[28]

Being largely unskilled and poor, the Irish clustered in the poorest areas of Wrexham. Most earned their living as agricultural labourers, hawkers and rag-gatherers. They were to be found, by now, scattered through about thirty streets of the town. The greatest concentration of Irish was to be found in Yorkshire Square, where there were about sixty adults, half of them lodgers and forty-one children, the number of children ranging between two and six per family.

Living conditions in parts of Wrexham before the incorporation of the town in 1857, were filthy and unhealthy. In a report to the Board of Health in 1850, on the state of the town, the inspector singled out Yorkshire Square as being especially bad:

> Here are altogether 35 tenements with one privy and that in a state quite unapproachable. The court is occupied by dung pits and collections of filth and in parts sodden with ordure. The privy of these cottages drains into a succession of open pools of soil which extend at the back of other cottages and into a public way opening from Tuttle Street. The sickness here is severe.[29]

Looking more closely at some of the Irish Catholic families in Yorkshire Square, we find William McNulty (aged thirty-one years) at N°. 6, a traveller in spectacles and his wife, Bridget. Both had been born in County Mayo in the west of Ireland, while their three small children had been born in Wrexham. Edward Donniher (aged fifty years) lived at N°. 9, a rag-gatherer, with his wife and two sons, all born in Sligo. Lodging with them were William and Bridget Dixon (both aged thirty) and their two children. At N°. 15 lived John Manning (aged fifty-seven) an agricultural labourer with his wife, Bridget and their son, John, a painter, born in London. Michael and Honor Kelly, in their mid-twenties lived at N°. 19. Their two young children had both been born in Wrexham. At N°. 20 lived Bernard Judge, an agricultural labourer (aged fifty-one) with his wife, Winifred (aged thirty-six) and their three children all born in Ireland. Lodging with them was Martin Quin, a tailor, his wife, Sarah (aged thirty-seven) and two young children born in Ireland as well as Michael Dixon (aged forty) and his wife Cisley (also aged forty) and three-month old Judy, born in Wrexham. John Hoban, wheelwright (aged fifty-four) lived at N°. 21, with Ann, his wife and son, Patrick (aged twenty-six), an agricultural labourer and seventeen-year-old Eleanor described as a dressmaker. She had been born in Bath, Somerset. Luke O'Neill, an agricultural labourer (aged twenty-six) lived with his twenty-four year old wife, Bridget at N°. 23 Yorkshire Square with three-year-old William. They had a visitor on census night, Bridget O'Hara (aged forty-eight), possibly Bridget's mother. At N°. 24 Yorkshire Square lived John Fagan (aged forty-four) with Anne his wife, a Wrexham woman, whose maiden name had been Owens. Their son, Thomas (aged twenty) was a skinner and had been born in Newcastle, while their daughter, Elizabeth (aged seventeen) was Wrexham-born.

All of these families had some contact with St David's Chapel, at least having had their children baptised there. Of the other Irish people in Yorkshire Square, we do not know whether they were practising Catholics or not, as their names do not appear in any of the church registers. It is quite clear that many of these families had travelled throughout the country in search of work and they may have been married and had their children baptised in different places.

But not all of the Irish were poor. John Beirne, though Irish, was born in Chester and came to Wrexham as a boy. Described by Dodd as the 'chief pillar of the cause' (i.e. Catholicism in Wrexham), he built up successful grocery, chandlery and brewing businesses.[30] Later, he owned the Albion Brewery on Town Hill. He was a benefactor of the Catholic school, which in the 1860s, he housed temporarily in his home, Mount House, while the new school in Brook Street was being erected. Later, he moved to a fine new property, Derwen, in the newly-developed Sontley Road. It has since been demolished. He was organist at St Mary's for thirty-two years and a long standing member of the Town Council. In 1876, he was to become the first Catholic Mayor of Wrexham.

Then there were the McDermotts, also Irish. Henry McDermott had been born in Manchester and kept the White Lion public house in Mount Street, as well as being a stone-mason, employing five men by 1851. All of his five children were baptised at St David's. Patrick McDermott, his brother, was a marine store dealer, also living in Mount Street.

John Beirne. [A. N. Palmer Centre]

Married to Ann, all four of his children were baptised at St David's chapel. He came to Wrexham in 1849 and was engaged in horse-dealing and iron-founding and became a man of property. In 1871, he completed the reservoir at Oswestry and at the opening ceremony, proposed the toast to the Queen.[31]

Nor were all of Wrexham's Catholics Irish. Foremost among the congregation continued to be the Thompson family. John Thompson, now in his eighties, lived out at Cefn-y-bedd and Richard, by now a JP, lived with his wife Ellen and their twins, John and Mary-Ann at Stansty Hall. Richard had been instrumental in the building of St David's Chapel and would later build St Mary's at his own expense. It was said of him that he was 'much respected among his own class for his modest and unassuming demeanour and greatly loved among the poor for his many acts of charity. One leading trait in his character was that the good he did in this way should not be known beyond the circle of the recipients thereof. He was one of those who did good by stealth and blushed to find it fame — his lady was largely endowed with the same amiable and benevolent qualities. After her death, he retired to Weld Bank and lived there a life of quietude and seclusion, in which seclusion, however, he never forgot to remember the poor'.[32] By 1851, Richard was a Vice-President of the Wrexham Literary Institute. The institute was established for the 'promotion of useful skills among the inhabitants of Wrexham, especially young men.' It boasted a reading room, circulating library, classes for mutual improvement, popular lectures and concerts. Richard's interest undoubtedly reflects the values he held most dear.[33]

A cause of great joy in the town was the wedding of Mary-Ann, Richard's daughter, at St David's Chapel on 18 October 1851. The bridegroom was the Hon. Thomas Ffrench, of Castle Ffrench, County Galway, Ireland. It was a measure of the regard felt locally for both Richard and his father John, that, despite little warning of the event, 'a most efficient committee was formed and immediate preparations made to mark the esteem in which the family are held'. A public subscription raised enough money 'to enable all classers to participate in the festivities'.[34] Twenty sheep were provided by the Thompsons and a fat bullock by the members of the committee.

> The day was ushered in by the ringing of the bells of Wrexham, Gresford and the adjoining churches. In Wrexham, several triumphal arches were thrown across the streets and private residences were decorated with laurel. The Committee in three open carriages at 10 o'clock left the Lion Hotel and set off towards Stansty Hall to escort the bridal party to the Catholic Chapel. On the party entering the Chapel, the choir played 'Let us adore the glory of the Lord.[35]

Dinners were given in several inns of the town, the main one taking place at the Lion Hotel on Tuesday, 28 October , when R. M. Biddulph of Chirk Castle gave 'a liberal present of game for the occasion'. After the meal there were toasts to the Queen and the rest of the

Royal Family, followed by a 'bumper' toast to the bride and groom. 'The name of Thompson', said the speaker, 'is held in deep regard in this locality and I will add that it is not revered more than it deserves to be.' Not only the Thompsons but also the Irish race, of which the groom was a member, was met with the speaker's admiration, 'I know something of the character of Irishmen — a freer-hearted, a more noble people do not exist on the earth', he said. 'The proceedings did not terminate until a late hour. '[36] Possibly, it was the effect of a good dinner, but there seems to have been little Catholic or Irish predjudice on the part of these worthy Wrexham citizens. Then, the wealth, status and influence of the Thompsons may have had an influence. The living conditions of the Irish Catholics in their midst, though, were in sharp contrast and could be described as anything but noble.

Another local Catholic was Charles Bate of 133 Yorke Street. He was a member of the landed gentry family of Marchwiel, where he had been born. By 1851, he was a brewer employing three men. His wife, Eliza, had been born in Chester. They had three children.

Ann Pugh was a convert, married to Joseph, a bricklayer's labourer, and living at 80 Salop Road with their four children. At 100 Penybryn lived Edward Roberts, hatter, and his wife, Eliza, who both came from Oswestry. They had two children.[37] These were just a few of the people who fitted into St David's Chapel, with difficulty and for whom a new church was becoming a pressing necessity.

Richard Thompson, by now grown wealthy on iron, coal and land, on 28 March 1854 bought a few strips of land for £1,296 from Sir Watkin Williams Wynne in what was then described as Hope Street, a leafy lane en route for the newly-built railway station. Richard had inherited the wealth of his father, John, who had died in 1852 aged eight-four, having been hit by a train while riding his horse near Cefn-y-bedd.

On the same day as the purchase of the land, Canon John Reah took charge of the Mission at Wrexham.

'A Time for Building'

But there were other reasons than shortage of space that made a new church desirable. Along with Catholics in the rest of Britain, Wrexham's congregation must have found a greater confidence, especially since the Restoration of the Hierarchy in 1850. This meant that after 265 years, the Catholic Church in this country would have normal church government, with a bishop in each of the newly-created sees and with priests in his diocese responsible to him. They also needed a more fitting church in which to celebrate Mass. Mid-century saw a spate of church building by all denominations, dominated by the architecture of Augustus Welby Pugin. In an age influenced by the Romantic Movement, Pugin's neo-Gothic style of church architecture was all the rage and was favoured in particular by Rev. John Hall, Vicar General of Shrewsbury diocese, in which Wrexham lay. He had expressed the view that any designs for Catholic churches should be placed in the hands of Pugin. Perhaps he had influenced Richard Thompson in the choice of architect for the design of the new church. At any rate Richard went ahead with the building of the church in memory of his wife, Ellen, who had died of cholera on 21 November 1854, aged fifty-two.

The chapel's dedication to St David was abandoned and the new church was to be dedicated to Our Lady of Sorrows to whom Ellen Thompson had had a special devotion. This may have reflected Richard's feelings, too, having lost both wife and father within a couple of years.

The architect he chose for the church was Edward Welby Pugin, the son of Augustus Welby Pugin, who had died in 1852. At the age of only eighteen, Edward had found himself in charge of the practice, and had set about completing his father's work, including a project at Chirk Castle and Shrewsbury's Roman Catholic Cathedral, claiming by now to be Shrewsbury's diocesan architect.[38] This was completed about a year before he was to design the church of Our Lady of Sorrows, Wrexham, when he was only twenty-three years old. It was the only church in Wales designed by him.

Edward Welby Pugin, architect of St Mary's Cathedral.

Like his father, Edward was prone to depression and illness due to overwork. An inveterate traveller by rail, on 16 September 1856, he 'left Wellington at 1/2 past 12 for Wrexham, when I found the going most satisfactory. Left at 10m past 3 for Liverpool.'[39] Also, like his father, he would die of overwork in his early forties.

Wrexham people showed keen interest in the development of the new church and seem to have been very pleased with it. By the spring of 1856, the church was in the course of erection. Before its opening, the *Wrexham Advertiser* described it as 'the most beautiful object among the numerous edifices that have lately sprung up on the road to the railway station'.[40]

The builder, Hugh Yates of Everton, Liverpool, is understood to have presented the lowest tender. Stone from Minera Quarry was used in its building and it is thought that the eventual cost was about £5,000. Richard Thompson also endowed it with £100 per annum.[41] The presbytery, also designed by Edward Welby Pugin, was built at the same time as the church. Pugin's designs also grace its interior. Ornamental gardens were laid out surrounding the church. In those grounds, near the entrance to the church, stands the stone cross which was once atop the roof of St David's Chapel and marks the burial place of Fr. Browne in 1872.

In a lengthy account of the church's opening is an architectural description of the church:

> The church, dedicated to Our Blessed Lady, under the title of 'Our Lady of Dolours' is designed in the full decorated period of Gothic or Christian architecture and consists of nave, chancel, blessed Sacrament chapel, tower and two aisles which form a total length and breadth of 100ft by 48ft. The nave is divided from the aisles by five well-proportioned arches which are surmounted by clerestory windows of a circular form, which are again sub-divided by four quatrefoils. The chancel opens into the Blessed Sacrament Chapel, with a pillar supporting two richly wrought arches which vanish into the jambs and have a chaste and pleasing effect. On the epistle side of the altar is the sacristy which unites the chancel and aisles of the church with the presbytery and is fitted up with oak ambries and cedar fittings together with every other suitable convenience. The chancel and side chapel roofs are divided and sub-divided into panels by wrought and moulded ribs, which will eventually be enriched with religious emblems. The roof of the nave is supported on seven wrought chamfered principals between which moulded ribs divide each compartment into eight panels. The east window is raised sixteen feet from the ground.[42]

Bishop Francis Mostyn.

Notice was given in the local press that the church would be opened on Thursday, 19 November, to be followed by a public dinner at the Wynnstay Arms and an account appeared in the *Wrexham Advertiser* of the opening of 'this beautiful structure which has attracted so much attention and has caused so much admiration in the town'and was 'one of the most unique and beautiful specimens of church architecture in the Principality.' The church was almost full, admission being by ticket. Many tradesmen of the town and people from the surrounding district were present.

High Mass proceeded after the bishops of Liverpool and Shrewsbury and other clergy had processed to the sanctuary to the accompaniment of the psalm 'How lovely are Thy tabernacles O Lord of hosts.'

The Bishop of Liverpool, Dr Alexander Goss, preached, referring to the builder of the church, Richard Thompson, as a generous, modest and retiring character who refused to come there among them that day on that account.

The choir sang Haydn's Mass No. 2, in a most effective and pleasing manner.

At the dinner, toasts were given to the Pope and the Queen. Bishop Brown, bishop of the diocese, acknowledging the new church as an ornament to the town hoped that it would prove eminently useful in regard to its spiritual wants. 'Generations yet to come', he said, 'would have occasion to bless the name of Richard Thompson.'

This was a very joyful occasion, but was followed nine years later by a sad one. It was Richard Thompson's funeral. He had died on 5 May 1866 at Weld Bank, Chorley. After his wife died and he had set in motion the building of the church, he left the area and moved to Weld Bank, 'where he lived a life of quietude and seclusion'.[43] He had not even broken this seclusion by attending the opening of St Mary's.

His funeral was a very elaborate one. In the week following his death his body was placed in a chapel at Weld Bank, where it was visited by crowds of the poor, who prayed for him with a devotion which testified to their affection for him. On the following Monday, his body was removed to the church there, where a very large congregation gathered for the Office of the Church, before the long journey by rail to Wrexham.

Richard Thompson's body arrived at Wrexham station at 6.30 pm via Chester. 'Long before, a vast concourse of people had assembled to witness the procession from there to St Mary's Church. A handsome hearse, with four black horses had been provided by Mr Murless of the Wynnstay Arms. Followed by his friends and relatives, his body was received at the gates of the church by the Bishops of Shrewsbury and Newport, with other clergy.

The church had been draped in mourning and the lower windows shaded with black cloth. The capitals and statues were covered in black crèpe. At 8pm began the Office of Matins of the Dead and the body was watched throughout the night. At the Mass the next

St Mary's Pro Cathedral and Presbytery, photographed c.1907. This picture gives a clear image of the formal gardens which surrounded the buildings at that time.

day, there were thirty clergy present and Bishop Browne of Newport preached.

> Afterwards, the clergy processed down the nave to the porch and thence to the vault.' Lately constructed by the deceased for the sacred resting place of his beloved wife, whose remains were removed hither a few months ago from St John's, Chester and placed on a marble slab on the left side of the entrance to the vaults — on the right and on a corresponding slab were finally deposited amid the deep lamentations and sympathy of many hundreds of mourning spectators, the earthly remains of this good Christian gentleman, the founder of this very beautiful church, of which this town is justly proud. Of himself and his beneficence to the poor and kindly charities, all in this immediate neighbourhood, without distinction of creed or race the sacred memory will long live with and be revered by all classes of Christians.[44]

By 1898, St Mary's was the pro-Cathedral for the new diocese of Menevia, a latinised form of that of St David's see — Mynyw, Bishop Francis Mostyn becoming its first bishop. Since 1895, he had been Bishop of the Vicariate of Wales. A member of the old catholic family, the Mostyns of Talacre, Wales, and especially north Wales, was very dear to his heart. The Catholic population of the diocese was something over 8,000. On Christmas day of that year, the first Pontifical High Mass in north Wales since the Reformation was celebrated. PhilipYorke of Erddig kindly provided evergreens to decorate the church.

Overleaf: The original chancel as designed by Pugin. Photographed c.1907.

Mater Dolorosa + Ora pro Nobis

Overleaf: The original nave as designed by Pugin. Photographed c.1907.

With Wrexham now part of the new diocese and with its bishop living in their midst, the Catholic community had come a long way in 100 years.

References

1. DODD, A. H., *The Industrial Revolution in North Wales,* 1950.
2. ROGERS, Emlyn. 'The history of trade unionism in the coalmining industry in North Wales to 1914', *DHST,* v.12, 1963.
3. BOSSY, John, *The English Catholic Community, 1570–1850,* DLT, 1975.
4. Copy address to the King concerning the late proposed Catholic Bill, 1807, DRO/ BD/A/70 .
5. DRO/PD/101/1/260A.
6. St Edmund's Archive.
7. CRS III, Holywell Registers.
8. FRO, Quarter Sessions, 12 January 1792.
9. Wrexham Diocesan Archives, Lennon MS, 1874.
10. Ibid.
11. Clifton Diocesan Archives, Letter Book.
12. Ibid.
13. Ibid.
14. Ibid.
15. Sir William Lloyd of Bryn Estyn, Pt 2, *DHST*, v.26, 17–19.
16. Wrexham Diocesan Archives, Lennon MS, 1874.
17. *Shrewsbury Chronicle,* 4 July 1828.
18. DOCKERY, *Collingridge: a Franciscan Contribution to Catholic Emancipation,* 1954.
19. *Shrewsbury Chronicle,* ibid.

Overleaf: The original Lady Chapel as designed by Pugin. Photographed c.1907.

20. Clifton Diocesan Archives Letter Book.
21. Holywell Confirmation Book.
22. NLW Visitation, 1841.
23. 1841 Census.
24. Ibid.
25. Shrewsbury Diocesan Archives, letter from Bishop Brown to Bishop Briggs, 16 May 1841.
26. NLW Visitation, 1841.
27. Laity's Directory, 1842.
28. 1851 Census and Parish Registers.
29. CLARKE, George T., *Report of the General Board of Health on a preliminary into the condition of Wrexham*, 1850.
30. DODD, A. H. (ed), *A History of Wrexham*, Bridge Books, 1989, p170.
31. JONES, Peter, 'The Irish in North-East Wales, 1851–1881' PhD Thesis, Manchester.
32. *Wrexham Advertiser*, 19 May 1866.
33. Ibid, 1 February 1851.
34. Ibid, 1 November 1851.
35. Ibid.
36. Ibid.
37. 1851 Census and parish registers.
38. *The Tablet*, 1866, p549.
39. Diary House of Lords Library.
40. *Wrexham Advertiser*, 12 September 1857.
41. *The Builder*, 29 March 1856 and 5 December 1857.
42. *Wrexham Advertiser*, 21 November 1857.
43. Ibid, 19 May 1866.
44. Ibid.

CHAPTER FIVE

St Mary's and its Development

The church building itself bears silent witness to some of those over the years who have worshipped within its walls, while the many additions to the original structure testify to the growth of the Catholic community over 150 years. Furthermore, as time has gone on, it has increasingly been altered and embellished and the future will doubtless see further change.

Towards the end of the nineteenth century, the Rector and Administrator 'took up with much zeal the work of supplementing the requirements of the pro-Cathedral by erecting a finely finished new altar. The design for this altar, as also for the Bishop's throne and the pulpit were drawn by Mr Peter Paul Pugin'.[1]

In the cloister there is a tomb and effigy of Ellen Thompson, wife of the founder. Carved in alabaster, it is said to have been executed by a self-taught sculptor. Until 1982, the tomb was situated near the entrance to the church, fittingly beneath a stained-glass window depicting the burial of Jesus, for just beneath is a vault containing the remains of both Richard and Ellen Thompson.

Numerous stained-glass windows have been incorporated into the building over the years in memory of local Catholics. Most of them were erected between 1908 and 1911 in Canon Quinn's time and they were produced by Hardman & Co of Birmingham.[2] The windows in the body of the church, in a clockwise direction from the entrance door, read as follows:

> Pray for J. H. Bate and his wife Winefride and their family. John Henry Bate was a local solicitor. Two Sisters of the Immaculate Conception, (or Holy Family), Srs. Mary Augustine and Sr. Mary Regis are commemorated by a pair of windows depicting Sts. Brigid and Patrick.

Tomb of Ellen Thompson.

The next window, which may have originally been in the sanctuary, depicting St Ann and St Thomas, was placed there in memory of Mary-Ann, Lady Ffrench and her husband, Lord Ffrench. Mary-Ann, Lady Ffrench, 1828–1906, was the daughter of Richard Thompson, who married Thomas, Lord Ffrench of

Castle Ffrench, County Galway, Ireland in 1851.

'During the Rectorship of Rev. N. Bickerton-Jones ... Lady Ffrench ... by her munificence placed over the High Altar a very artistic stained-glass window, representing Our Lady of Sorrows with the dead body of her Divine Son in her lap ...[3] The Cathedral is dedicated to Our Lady of Sorrows and the window depicts her surrounded by Saints David and Winefride, four Archangels and other saints — St Winefride (virgin, martyr), St Thomas (apostle), St Michael (Archangel), St Gudwal (sixth century missionary-bishop), St Raphael (Archangel), St Urel (Archangel), St Keyna (sixth century virgin, well-known in south Wales) and St Gabriel (Archangel).

The rose window above the altar.

The windows depicting SS Richard and Helena in the south aisle read:

> Pray for the soul of Richard Thompson and pray for the soul of Ellen Thompson, the founder of the church and his wife

The next windows depict SS David and Winefride and request prayers for the souls of John and Jane Beirne. John Beirne, Mayor of Wrexham in 1876, was organist at St Mary's for thirty-two years. The next pair of windows depict SS Hugh and Margaretta of Scotland, and request prayers for Hugh Nelson and his wife, Mary.

A window set up in memory of Charles and Eliza Bate, depicts St Charles Borromeo and St Elizabeth. Charles, a member of the Bate family of Marchwiel, was a well-known brewer. The last window on the south aisle requests prayers 'for the welfare, both spiritual and temporal for the generous donor of this window.' Adjacent to this, is a window depicting the Apparition of Our Lady of Lourdes, marking the priestly Jubilee in 1909 of Bishop Mostyn, Bishop of Menevia, 1898–1921.

To the left of the main entrance to the cathedral is a window showing the burial of Jesus. This is very fitting, for beneath it used to stand the tomb of Ellen Thompson and in a vault beneath rest both her remains and those of her husband, Richard.

In what is now the cloister is a window, near the tomb of Ellen Thompson, depicting the Resurrection, while the next shows St Frances of Rome and St Peter, with a request to 'Pray for the soul of Sir Pyers Mostyn, 8th baronet, and his wife the Honorable Georgiana Mostyn.' They were members of an old Catholic family, who had remained true to the Catholic faith from the time of the Reformation. They were the parents of Bishop Francis Mostyn, DD, Bishop of Menevia at the time the windows were installed.

In the Blessed Sacrament chapel, which was at the time the Lady Chapel are a pair of windows dedicated to St Agnes, 'pray for the young girls of this mission' and to St Edward, ' Pray for the soul of Mgr Edward Slaughter.' A cousin of Bishop Mostyn, Mgr Slaughter

The Bate memorial window.
[Dr Matthew Byrne]

The Beirne memorial window.
[Dr Matthew Byrne]

The window depicting the burial of Jesus.
[Dr Matthew Byrne]

The Nelson memorial window.
[Dr Matthew Byrne]

The Richard Gwyn memorial window.

was administrator of the pro-Cathedral, 1895–1900. The next window of three lights portrays the Way of the Cross.

In the same chapel, we find a window with figures of SS Francis and Clare. These request prayers for 'William Hope Nelson and his wife Doris Violet nee Knipe', who lived at Acton Hall, which was leased to them by the Cunliffes. By 1912, the Nelson family were owners of the world's largest fleet of reefer ships, engaged in the carriage of meat from Argentina to Britain. As well as the ships, the Nelson family owned freezer works in South America and retail butcher shops in this country, which numbered some 1,500 by the time the retail interests were sold to Vestey's in 1913.[4]

The St Richard Gwyn window in what is now the Lady Chapel was designed and executed by Pamela Bubb, a student at the nearby College of Art in 1981. The glass is German Antique and Hetley Hartley Woods Antique, all in mouth-blown sheet glass with painted pigment and applied lead. Adjacent to the window, the painting behind the pieta was executed at about the same time by Sue Moore, also a student at the College of Art.[5]

By the 1950s, it was felt that Wrexham's Catholic martyr should have a shrine in the cathedral. Opposite the Richard Gwyn window, but predating it, is the St Richard Gwyn Shrine. A relic of the saint, an arm-bone, was the gift of the Jesuits at Manresa College, Roehampton in 1952. Bows and Bartlett were commissioned to make a case for it and a reliquary fifteen-inches high and electro-gilt with ebonized hardwood gallows with electro-gilt lettering was purchased from the Art Bookshop for £248 15*s*. Fred Roberts, an architect and a Mold parishioner, designed the grille protecting the shrine.[6]

To celebrate the Millenium in 2000, Sr. Petra Clare was commissioned to create an icon of St Richard Gwyn, who had been canonised on 25 October 1970. He is depicted with nine scenes from his life and death. The icon was blessed by Bishop Edwin Regan on Sunday, 16 October 2000 and has been placed near the martyr's shrine. Sr. Petra is a Benedictine nun, who lives and works in a monastic skete [small monastery] in the Scottish Highlands.[7] The icon of Our Lady of Czestochowa was a gift from Wrexham's Polish community in the 1980s.

Near the confessional can be seen a plaque in memory of David Lord, Wrexham town's only recipient of the Victoria Cross. It reads 'Of your charity pray for the soul of FLT/LT DAVID S. A. LORD, VC, DFC, RAF killed in action at Arnhem 19th Sep 1944, formerly an altar server in this church.' Arriving back from India, where his father had served with the

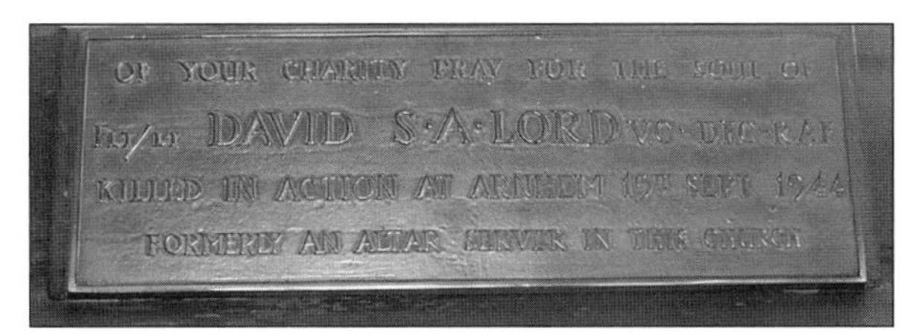

Flt/Lt David Samuel Anthony Lord, VC, DFC and his memorial plaque close to the confessional. [W. Alister Williams Collection]

Royal Welsh Fusiliers, David attended St Mary's School. Considering a vocation to the priesthood, he studied at St Mary's College, Aberystwyth before going to the English College in Valladolid, Spain, which he left in 1934. In 1936, he enlisted in the RAF. By 1942, he was commissioned as a pilot officer, being awarded the DFC in the following year for his services in re-supplying Chindit units in the Burmese jungle. He took part in the D-Day operations in June 1944 and in the Arnhem operations the following September. He was killed in action over Arnhem on 19 September 1944, for which he was awarded the Victoria Cross, 'By continuing his mission in a damaged and burning aircraft, descending to drop the supplies accurately, returning to the dropping zone a second time and, finally remaining at the controls to give his crew a chance to escape, Flight Lieutenant Lord displayed supreme valour and self sacrifice.'[8]

The organ, costing £400, built by Messrs Gray and Davidson, was opened on 15 July 1860 and the bell was cast by Murphy of Dublin. It cost £200, which was raised by public subscription and it was placed in the belfry in 1864.[9]

The Stations of the Cross in oil were erected and blessed in 1906, from a legacy of £100 left by Richard Thompson for that purpose, while a large crucifix was placed above the pulpit in 1909. Both pulpit and crucifix have since been removed.

Alterations and Extensions

St Mary's was not built as a cathedral, but as a parish church of the then diocese of Shrewsbury, hence its small size. Over the years, as the Catholic community of Wrexham increased, extra facilities were needed. Furthermore, following the Second Vatican Council, the new liturgy required a re-ordering of the sanctuary. All of this means that the church has been in a constant state of repair, development and embellishment, which continues today.

During Mgr Nightingale's time, 1913–47, the church was decorated and restored three or four times. The spire was found to be out of true and had to be taken down and built up again.[10] In 1957, the church's centenary year, the church was enlarged. Architect Fred Roberts 'designed a new altar, planned the new sacristies and porch together with alterations to sanctuary and side chapels'.[11] A new Lady Chapel was incorporated two years later.

There was another major extension of the church in 1966, when a new chapel to

Mgr Nightingale and two priests with members of the Cathedral Choir, c.1945.

accommodate 100 and costing £18,500 was added onto the porch. Canon Evans, the Administrator, said 'the Cathedral could cope with the normal Sunday congregation of about 1,000, but beyond that it is a bit of a squeeze.' The congregation had grown over the years, he said. Asked whether this indicated a large number of converts to Catholicism, he said that there had been some, but the increase was largely due to natural growth of families and an influx into the area of Catholics. It was during the sixties that the pro-Cathedral began to be known as the Cathedral. By the 1980s, it was found that 'the church needed new central heating, while the presbytery was in need of a substantial overhaul.' Accompanying this announcement in the Sunday Bulletin was the inevitable appeal for generosity on the part of the congregation.[12]

Other Buildings

The Presbytery, now known as Clergy House, also designed by Edward Welby Pugin, was built at the same time as the church. Pugin's designs also grace the interior of the house. In the early 1990s, because of subsidence, major work had to be undertaken on the Presbytery and the whole structure had to be underpinned. As a result of the subsequent renovation, an original Pugin fireplace was revealed in the dining room.[13]

Mgr Nightingale..

Ornamental gardens were laid out surrounding the church. In those grounds, near the entrance to the church, is a stone cross, which was once atop St David's Chapel in King Street and marks the last resting place of Fr. Edward Francis Browne, rector of Wrexham, 1857–72.

In the wider community, the development of Wrexham meant, more than once, that Regent Street was required to be widened and this gradually encroached on the gardens surrounding St Mary's. This meant that the proportions were no longer as pleasing and eventually, as more people owned cars, much of what had been garden became the car park we know today.[14]

St Mary's Church Hall, then known as St Mary's Institute, was opened by Sir William Nelson, Bt. of Acton Park, in Easter Week, 1911. It was built to meet the needs of the younger people of the parish and consisted of a large well-ventilated billiard room, a committee room for the meetings of the Society of St Vincent de Paul, who had charge of the Institute

The nave and chancel as it was configured before 1957.

St Mary's Cathedral (left) under a heavy fall of snow in the 1950s.The church on the right is St Mark's which was demolished in1959. A substantial part of the grounds was taken as part of a road widening scheme in the 1960s.

and a very fine spacious Assembly Room for public meetings etc for the congregation and their friends. Under the building there was a miniature rifle range.[15] In 1957, Canon Adolph Evans, Administrator of the pro-Cathedral, remarked, 'Wrexham parish is one big family. Its social side is helped by the fact that it enjoys a magnificent hall — one of the best parochial halls in the Principality, built by the generosity of the parishioners — many of them very poor — under the late Very Rev. Canon John Quinn.'[16]

In order to bring more social life for the men of the parish, in Coronation year, 1953, St Mary's Club was built, with a number of parishioners working until nine or ten o'clock at night to erect it. One of the curates, Fr. Schwarz was the driving force behind it. Reg Sumner was to be the Club's first president.

In the new Millenium, work continues to be done to repair and restore the church. Electrical work had to be undertaken in the summer of 2002, when it was found to be in a dangerous condition and there are plans to re-wire and re-light the building after fifty years. The following year, faults in the stonework of the spire were identified, with the recommendation that the top third of the spire be taken down and rebuilt. This work is

Above: The nave and chancel as reconfigured in 1957.

Right: The new Lady Chapel (with the altar that previously stood in the chancel), built in 1959. [Dr Matthew Byrne)

Overleaf: The view from the Sanctuary, late 1960s.

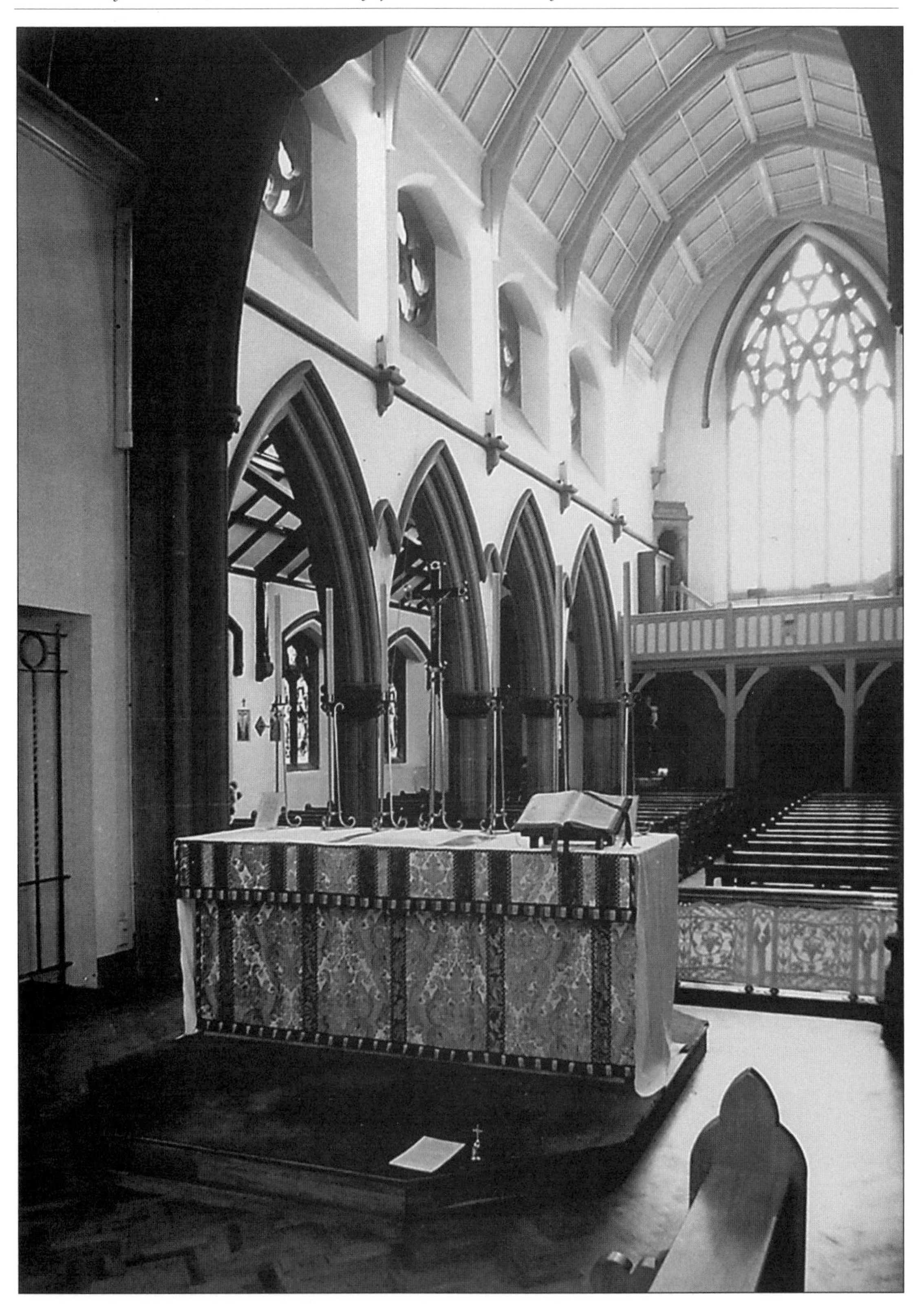

The Sanctuary in 1999. [Dr Matthew Byrne]

underway at the present time and will probably take about four months of a specialist mason's time and skill. Fundraising is going on. 'The support from the diocese has been considerable and it is most heartening that the people across north Wales are willing to contribute to the repair and maintenance of their Cathedral' says the Dean, Fr. Peter Brignall. Bishop Regan, in the summer of 2006 did a sponsored walk to Compostella, raising £24,000 to be shared between the Cathedral and the Lesotho Aids charity.

But, repairs apart, what are the plans for the future enhancement of the Cathedral? The present Dean, Fr. Peter Brignall, has commented:

> We have plans to try to restore something of the Victorian splendour of the church which was destroyed in the 1950s. However, much of the original decoration was not just painted over, but sanded away first and the original fixtures, fittings and sanctuary furniture were totally removed and disposed of, the only original feature not being destroyed being the high altar, which is now the Blessed Sacrament altar — the reredos and other furniture have gone. When I was appointed, the Bishop asked me to begin the re-ordering and restoration of the sanctuary. That we shall begin in 2007, with the restoring of the Baptistry in the Cathedral, and the bringing back of the original font from its exile in the cloister. A Pugin pulpit will be restored to the chancel and will become the ambo. The general plan is to restore something of the Pugin character of the building's interior.

Other plans are to install some bells and to commission a stained-glass window in the

The Sacristy built in 1957.

cloister to commemorate the Reformation martyrs of north Wales, to whom no collective memorial exists.

So, as the twenty-first century develops, we can look back and take inspiration from those who have gone before, while being mindful of the legacy which we leave to those who worship in this building in the years to come.

References

1. Wrexham Diocesan Archives, Quinn MS, 1903.
2. Birmingham City Archives, Hardman & Company records.
3. Wrexham Diocesan Archives, Quinn MS, 1903.
4. Information kindly supplied by David Burrell.
5. From information supplied by Steve Hill, former lecturer at the College of Art, Wrexham.
6. Wrexham Diocesan Archives.
7. Leaflet 'Creating the icon of St Richard Gwyn' by the artist.
8. From his citation in the *London Gazette*, 13 November 1945. For the full citation see: WILLIAMS, Alister, *The Encyclopaedia of Wrexham*, 2001.
9. PALMER, A. N., *A History of the Town of Wrexham*, 2nd ed., 1982.
10. Memories of Mgr James Mulroy.
11. *Menevia Record*, November 1957.
12. *Sunday Bulletin*, 2 May 1982.
13. Canon Bernard Morgan's memories.
14. Wrexham Diocesan Archives.
15. 'The Catholic story of Wrexham', *Menevia Record*, November 1957.
16. EVANS, Canon A., 'St Mary's pro-Cathedral, 1947–1957', *Menevia Record*, November 1957.

CHAPTER SIX

The Twentieth Century and Beyond

By the early years of the new century, the number of Catholics in Wrexham was about 1,475.[1] The great event in the first decade was the consecration of the pro-Cathedral on 7 November 1907, by Bishop Mostyn. The solemnity coincided with the celebration of the church's Golden Jubilee.

Another mark of progress at about this time, was the formation of a Cathedral chapter, or body of canons, by order from Rome. Provost Ratcliffe was appointed with five canons, V. Revs Jennings, Griffiths, Kelly, Moore and McLoughlin.[2] By now the Missionary Rector at Wrexham, Fr. Quinn, set about embellishing the pro-Cathedral with stained glass windows in memory of prominent local Catholic families of the time including the Nelson family of Acton Park, whose daughter, Josephine, was married in the pro-Cathedral in 1908.

There were many activities in the parish. The congregation was treated to a lantern lecture in St Mary's Schools on 'Bruges and its pilgrimage' by Fr. Filmer in February 1909, while the following week saw a five-day Mission led by Fr. Jaggar, SJ, the subject being 'The Soul – its destiny – its defilement – its ruin – its awakening and its arraignment.'

In 1913, Fr. Quinn, who had served Wrexham since 1903, was transferred to Bangor, to be replaced by Fr., later Monsignor, George Nightingale who was to be the Administrator of the pro-Cathedral until 1947.

From 1914 to 1918, when Britain was at war with Germany, many young men of the parish would have gone to serve their country. At the outbreak of war, under the headline 'The War: Thrilling Scenes in Wrexham', the local paper described the streets thronged with people, eagerly waiting the latest news. There was widespread support and enthusiasm for the war, but among the 1,300 men mobilised by 8 August, a proportion would have been Catholics, never to see Wrexham again.[3]

Between the Wars

In Britain, the period between the two world wars was marked by industrial decline. By the 1920s, trade was unsettled and there was increasing unemployment, especially in the mining industry.

> One example of the poverty [in Wrexham] is a memory of local police officers providing boots and shoes for some children. Evidence of the poverty in existence during the 1920s and 30s was witnessed in another domain — the sight of men wheeling their bicycles laden with coalwaste from local colliery spoil tips.[4]

In St Mary's parish, there were increasing calls on the Society of St Vincent de Paul for relief. By 1927, the society had sixteen members and in his report for that year, the Secretary thanked their supporters who 'enabled the good work of bringing succour to God's poor in their hour of need'. The help given included groceries, boots, funeral expenses, tobacco and tea for inmates of the workhouse and spectacles for a poor girl [SVP Secretary's report 1927].[5]

By this time, average Sunday mass attendance was 693. The late Frank More was an altar server and remembered Mgr Nightingale being very strict. Boys admitted to be altar servers were examined in the Latin responses to the Mass, kneeling before him in his room. He was also a stickler for punctuality, checking the time on his gold pocket watch. When officiating at Sunday evening Benediction, he would recite not only the prayer for Wales but also the prayer for England, being a Yorkshire man.

The St Vincent de Paul Society was not the only organisation active in the parish. Various sodalities were introduced at this time. One of their requirements was the monthly reception of Holy Communion, only possible in those days at an early mass as there was no communion at the High Mass.

> In the late 1920s the Sacred Heart sodalities were established for men and women. Members received Holy Communion together at the appointed Sunday Mass and after Benediction recited the prescribed prayers. Nowadays the sodality members are few compared to its hey-day but until the 1990s prayers continued to be said after the 9 o'clock mass on the first Friday of each month.'

Frank More also remembers the Children of Mary:

> We had processions around the Cathedral one Sunday evening each May and on the Sunday following the Feast of Corpus Christi (Body of Christ). The sodalities took part. During the May procession, the statue of Our Lady was carried by four members of the Children of Mary, wearing white dresses and blue capes. In the Corpus Christi procession the Blessed Sacrament was carried in a monstrance by the bishop or a priest. Benediction then followed with the prescribed Latin hymns being sung. The procession took place on the lawns between the flower beds, which have long since disappeared to provide a car park.[6]

The slump in industry was a feature of the 1930s. Miners only worked two or three days each week, a hooter sounding when they were not required for work. In 1934, Gresford Colliery was the scene of the worst disaster in the history of the north Wales coalfield, when 265 men lost their lives. A Requiem Mass was celebrated at the pro-Cathedral for the repose of their souls.[7]

By this time, an average of 787 were filling the pro-Cathedral each Sunday. Each October, Mr Byrne, the manager of the Maypole Stores is remembered as leading the Rosary. There was a Children's Mass at 9.30 on Sundays and the members of the Young Men's Sodality were required to recite their special Office every day. There was an annual outing led by Fr. Nolan, usually to Southport. Fr. Nolan is also remembered as preaching long sermons from the pulpit at Sunday evening service. The Knights of the Blessed Sacrament were also a feature of parish life at this tim

It was during the 1930s that Pope Pius XI promoted Catholic Action as a 'remedy for our present discontent in the troubled state of the post-war world.' He saw Catholic Action as 'the participation and collaboration of the laity with the Apostolic Hierarchy in matters affecting the rights and vital interests of Holy Mother Church.' It was envisaged that 'the numerous Catholic societies which exist in this country [would] … be linked in corporate unity [giving] a powerful organisation for moulding public opinion and for asserting and defending our Catholic rights.' Catholics were urged to enrol in the National Council for Catholic Action under the patronage of the Hierarchy of England and Wales, following the example shown by Westminster's Catholic Federation'.[8] The SVP continued to do good work, backed financially by the congregation so that they could 'continue to support and enable timely aid to be granted to God's poor'.[9] A further feature of the 1930s were the Old Folks' Treat and the school-children's outing.

Fund-raising was as essential a part of parish life in the 1930s as it is now. Familiar names on the Church Renovation Fund Subscription List 1933–4 were Mackreth, McMahon, Lord and Beirne, while there were also donations from the Children of Mary and from the choir.[10]

The Sewing Meeting were busy in 1931 preparing for the Sale of Work and Garden Fete [to be one of many] which took place in St Mary's Institute and grounds on 10 June from 2.30 pm to 8.00 pm. It was opened by the Archbishop of Cardiff, Francis Mostyn. Its principle object, according to the printed programme was to assist in raising funds to provide the necessary extensions to St Mary's Schools in Lea Road. The many stalls included household linens, women's garments and men's and boys' wear organised by the Women's Sodality, Mrs McDermott's china and glass stall, girls' frocks and fancy work supervised by the Children of Mary, a fruit and flower stall organised by the staff from St Mary's School and a miscellaneous stall arranged by staff from the Convent School. There were the usual refreshments and entertainments in the grounds followed by a dance and cabaret in the evening at a cost of 1*s.* 6*d.*.[11]

On a more serious note, from time to time there were missions, which were very popular, despite — or perhaps because of — their 'hell-fire' sermons Fr. Daniel Collier, OMI (Oblates of Mary Immaculate) and Fr. Michael Fitzpatrick, OMI, a missionary order long contributing to the life of the diocese, gave a two-week mission in January, 1931. The Redemptorist Fathers preached a mission in 1939. Frank More remembers, 'There were "packed houses" and additional chairs had to be brought in from St Mary's Hall and placed in the middle aisle. Men and boys sat on the High Altar steps and the overspill sat in what was then the Lady Chapel.'[12]

During the decade, the number of Catholics attending Sunday Mass at St Mary's pro-Cathedral on Sundays was on the increase and by 1937, the diocese was looking for land on which to build a second church. There was land available at Borras Road and by early 1939, plans were drawn up for a new church to be built there to accommodate 342 people. Presumably, it was the war that intervened and it was not until 1949 that the plans were looked at again.[13]

Wartime, 1939–45

By the outbreak of war, the Catholic population of Wrexham was over 2,000.[14] This number was to decline as men went off to join the services, but other Catholics came into the area, principally evacuees from Liverpool and Birkenhead. Over 600 children, 446 of them under fourteen years of age, came into the parish. Provision had to be made for them in a variety of ways. The effects of this were mostly felt in the school, where the pupils of St Anne's School, Liverpool had to be accommodated. A shift system operated, St Mary's pupils going to school in the morning and those of St Anne's attending in the afternoon.[15] Jim Angus was one of those who came as an evacuee and stayed on, later to teach science at Victoria School.[16]

A group of parishoners in the 1940s.

During the war, midnight Mass at Christmas was discontinued and it was arranged that in the event of an air raid that the pro-Cathedral would be open day and night, a priest being on hand to give the sacraments of Penance and Eucharist for all who asked for them. Parishioners were urged to spend time there in prayer in penitence for sin, national as well as personal and above all in repentance for the corporate sin of war.[17]

Despite the war, activities in the parish continued. There were social afternoons, with whist and refreshments. The sewing and knitting class produced items for the Sale of Work, where Mr McMahon continued to have a fruit and vegetable stall and Mr McDermott a china and brass stall, while Miss Cafferly sold her baby clothes. Bella Marubbi had an apron stall, and her husband, owner of the café in Bank Street, ran a grocery stall.[18]

By this time, the town of Wrexham was growing apace as its boundaries were extended and the population increased. This situation prompted the diocese to look again at the possibility of a second parish in Wrexham. In 1943, it was planned to build a new church on Borras Road, but this plan came to nothing. The development of the Queens Park estate may have affected this.[19] Meanwhile, the Rydal Chapel at Coedpoeth was purchased for £110 in 1949 to serve the Catholics in that area, and was opened on 11 June 1950 under the title of the Holy Family.[20]

The consecration of Bishop John Petit took place on 25 March 1947 in Llandudno, and he would serve the diocese for twenty-five years. At this time, Mgr Nightingale, Administrator of the pro-Cathedral, retired to Rotherham on the grounds of ill-health. So there began a new chapter in both parish and diocese. 1949 saw the end of yet another chapter when Florence Ellis, who had been organist for many years, tendered her resignation.[21]

In the late 1940s and 1950s, British people were to experience a period of austerity, rebuilding and recovery after six years of war. In the parish too, this time was marked by development and expansion. The Catholic population of Wrexham was again rising, with nearly 800 people attending Mass on a Sunday, filling the church four times. The increase was brought about by wartime evacuees staying on, through conversion and through English and Polish Catholics buying farms in the countryside around Wrexham, as more and more took advantage of recent legislation favouring agriculture.[22]

A large number of Poles settled in Britain after the war, having undergone the trauma of war — imprisonment, concentration camps, deportation and deprivation of many kinds. Many came to the Wrexham area, some living in the Polish hospital at Penley. Initially, after living there or in other settlement camps, jobs were found and homes made in the area. 'Most of us were Catholics and from the very beginning our association with Wrexham Cathedral was central to our culture. Getting to know the people of Wrexham was important to enable us to settle happily in this area,' says Irena Szenderowicz, affectionately known as 'Mother of the Poles.' In 1989, a monument was raised in Wrexham Cemetery, 'in memory of the Polish soldiers and their families to whom the return to free Poland was not given and who are buried here and in other cemeteries in Wales.' The Polish community gradually diminished over the years, but Wrexham parish remained important to them. For them, St Mary's Cathedral and St Mary's Hall have been the centre of religious and social activities, marriages, christenings, first communions, confirmations and funerals. Mass was celebrated by a Polish priest once a month for many years and this played an important part in holding the community together. Just as the numbers of Poles in Wrexham were declining, there was a new influx as a result of Poland joining the EU in 2004, and there are now about 5,000 Poles in the area. A weekly Mass in Polish is provided to serve their needs.[23]

Many Italian Catholics also came into the area; some prisoners of war simply stayed on. They came from all over Italy, seeking work and each other's company and friendship. Giovanni Battista Cargius, father of Rosanna Jones, settled here in the early 1950s, joining his elder brother, who had been a prisoner of war. He had stayed on after the war, as work was in short supply in Calabria, where he came from. Rosanna's father was a mechanic by

Bishop Petit with the Ladies Sodality, 1945/6.

Mgr Nightingale with the Men's Sodality, mid 1940s.

trade, but most Italians found work on farms. Rosanna's mother, Chiarina Pansera came to join him in 1954. From poor beginnings, they worked hard together, having five children. With others in the area, they formed a vibrant Italian community. 'Like Italian communities in all parts of the world, they were to bring their many gifts and attributes, warmth, colour, hospitality, that will not be beaten anywhere else in the world,'says Rosanna Jones.[24]

There was a crying need to support Catholic schools and it was during the post-war years that the Catholic Parents and Electors Association was set up throughout the diocese with this in mind.

Its objectives were:

> to learn and teach the duties and rights of parents;
>
> to promote and safeguard Catholic educational interests and the care of Catholic youth;
>
> to encourage representation of Catholic parents on public educational bodies;
>
> to encourage the practice of family prayers in every Catholic household of the parish.

Mr Eric McMahon and Mrs M. Fletcher, both of the pro-Cathedral parish, were members of the Diocesan Council. Mrs J. Sullivan, a teacher at St Mary's School, was the Secretary of the Area Council in Denbighshire. The branch chairman of Wrexham and Llay was Mr W. T. Crosland-Taylor, while Mr F. H. Moore was its secretary.[25]

By the mid twentieth century, the Catholic Church in this country was growing in confidence. An example of this was seen on 13 June 1947, the Feast of the Sacred Heart, when Mass was sung publicly at Valle Crucis Abbey, near Llangollen — for the first time since the Reformation — on the occasion of the first International Eisteddfod. The following day, Cistercians from Mount St Bernard Abbey in Leicestershire processed solemnly into the abbey, a Cistercian foundation dating from 1201. High Mass on the Sunday, to complete the Triduum, (the three days of rejoicing) on account of the inclement weather, was celebrated at the pro-Cathedral. Many must have happy memories of that day — the entry of the ministers of the Mass into the ruined abbey and the slow march of the Cistercian fathers through the fields to the west door of the church. People had travelled long distances 'to

The wedding group photograph of two senior members of the congregation in the 1940s.

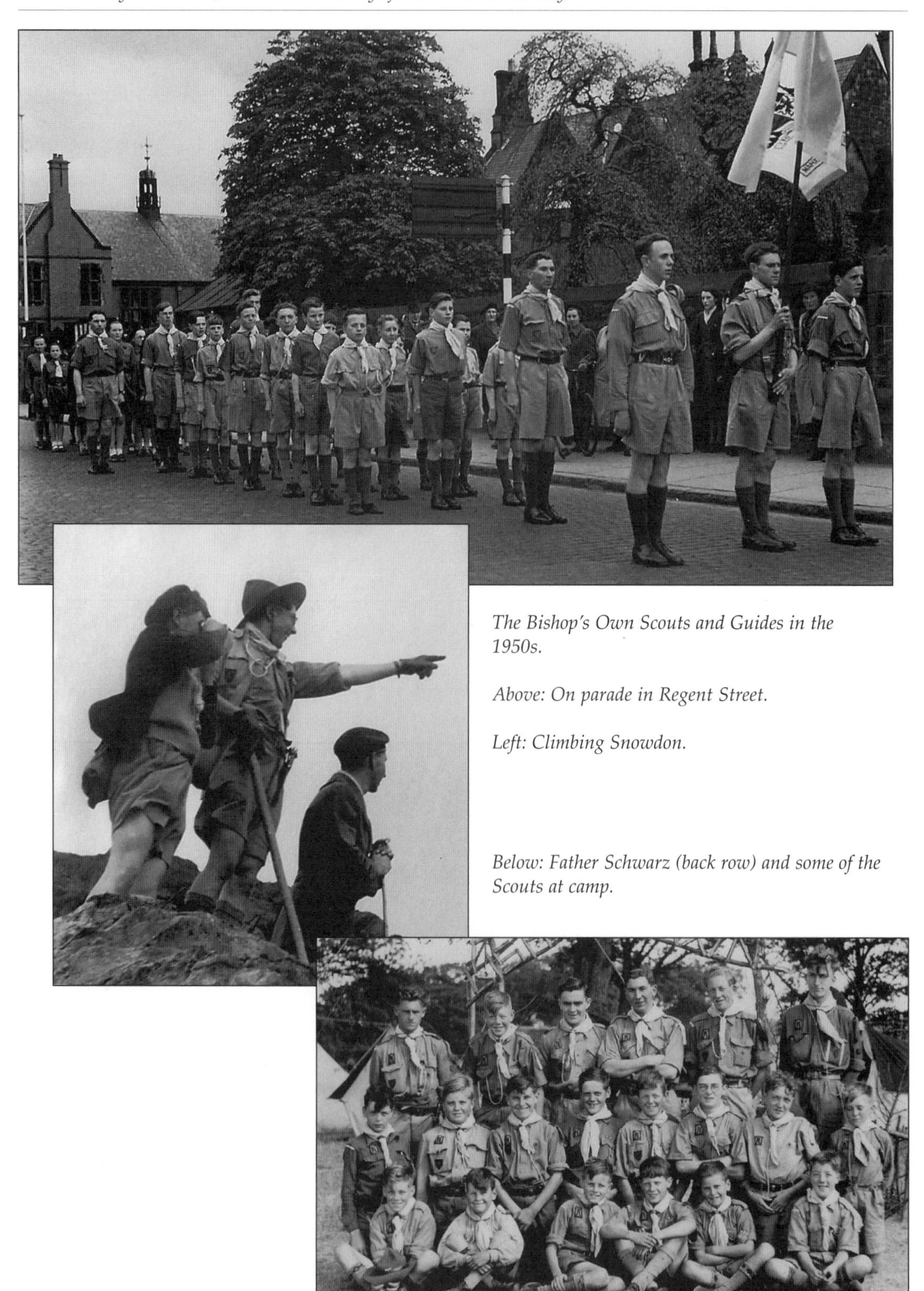

The Bishop's Own Scouts and Guides in the 1950s.

Above: On parade in Regent Street.

Left: Climbing Snowdon.

Below: Father Schwarz (back row) and some of the Scouts at camp.

witness the return of the Mass and the Divine Office to a valley which had been silent for centuries'.[26]

Wrexham continued to expand and by this time, there were plans to develop a new estate on the east side of the town, to be known as Queen's Park. The Council approached Bishop Petit to see whether the diocese would require a site for a church. The Bishop, replying in the affirmative, said that at least five acres would be required for church, presbytery and a school.[27]

It was in 1947 that Fr. Adolph Evans was appointed Administrator of the pro-Cathedral, a post he held until his death in 1982. One of his curates was Fr. Cyril Schwarz, a zealous priest, who was to be responsible for many initiatives. One of these, which would influence the lives of many Catholic boys in the area, was the formation of the Bishop's Own Scout Troop in February, 1948.

> The numbers were small to begin with, but as the news got around, more boys joined and soon there were four patrols. Lack of equipment did not prevent them enjoying the outdoor life of scouting. No troop camp was possible in the first year, but many of the scouts camped at Llangollen or Carrog with brother scouts from Liverpool and Oswestry. Later that year, the Guides were formed, bringing a spirit of competition.[28]

The following year, a large number of patrol camps and Guide hikes were held and the Guides camped at Caernarfon in 1949, while the Scouts camped at Gwrych Castle for a fortnight when the Welsh Scout Jamboree was being held. By the time of the Christmas party in 1949, there were over ninety Scouts, Guides, Cubs and Brownies.

The first organised pilgrimage to leave Wales for Lourdes, set off from Wrexham Station in September, 1949. Both Scouts and Guides took part and helped with the sick. 'The singing of the Lourdes hymn rang through Wrexham station'as sixty pilgrims set out.[29]

The 1950s

Every twenty-five years since 1450, the popes have proclaimed the Holy Year of Jubilee, when Catholics have been encouraged to travel to Rome in a spirit of pilgrimage. The year 1950 was proclaimed a Holy Year by Pope Pius XII and thousands of pilgrims made their way to Rome for the Jubilee. Seven members of the Bishop's Own Scout Troop from

Bishop's Own Wolf Cub Pack, 1959.

Girl Guides and Brownies, c.1970.

Scouts football team, 1950s.

Scout Gang Show, 1970s.

Bishop Petit with priests, altar servers and choir, 1950s.

Wrexham were among the 1,200 British Scouts who headed for the Eternal City. Back in Wrexham, Senior Scouts were formed and now housed themselves in an old stable behind the pro-Cathedral.[30]

In 1949, members of the Scouts and Guides, finding that they had no money to buy necessary equipment, decided to put on a pantomime to raise funds. This soon became an annual event. Canon Evans, painted some of the props himself, while Fr. Schwarz was the producer of the show. It went from strength to strength and over the years enabled the purchase of badly-needed tents and other items of camping equipment. 'Thus' said the *Wrexham Leader*, 'the scouts and guides are doing their bit to make Wrexham pantomime conscious, while at the same time they have found a profitable and entertaining way of spending the long winter nights.'

The liturgy of the Church has always been an important part of life at the pro-Cathedral. Mass and other services were, of course, in Latin in the 1950s and 1960s. Sr. Salome was in charge of the choir, 'at first an all-female affair mostly captured from the Convent High School. Later, it became a mixed choir. The choir was ambitious. They sang the Asperges from Easter to Whit. They also knew six plainchant Masses plus the *Missa de profundis*. Two credos as well as motets and anthems also formed part of their repertoire. The solemn entry of Bishop Petit through the main door of the pro-cathedral was regularly announced to the chant *Ecce sacerdos magnus* — a truly majestic occasion and very fitting for Bishop Petit. The most important service during Holy Week in those days was that of Tenebrae, which took place on the evenings of Wednesday, Thursday and Friday of Holy Week. His Lordship led the chants and the candles were extinguished to choral accompaniment.'[31]

Changes in the Mass were later to be the order of the day. The introduction of the Dialogue mass, remembered as the first innovation, caused little reaction in the parish. Esther McGivern remembers later, that all the many missals and prayer books in her family quickly became obsolete.

Father Schwarz (back row, centre) with First Communicants and families, 1950s.

It was in 1950 that the Bishop put forward Eric McMahon's name to be Justice of the Peace in Wrexham. Educated at St Mary's School and Grove Park, he was a fishmonger and poulterer. 'Old Mr McMahon,' his father, is remembered by Fr. Charles Lloyd as one of the many altar servers. 'A fishmonger and patriarch, he had come from Ireland before the First World War with a barrow selling fish — a self-made, lovely, humble man, he more often than not served first Mass on weekdays, dressed in black coat, striped trousers and, I think, a stand-up collar and formal tie. He was very devout, always wearing his Sunday best for his Lord.'

His son, Eric, was also active in the life of the church and he had been a member of the Borough Council since 1944. In 1952, he became Wrexham's second Catholic Mayor. On Mayor's Sunday, as reported in the *Wrexham Leader*, 'he broke with a ten-year-old tradition. Instead of the Civic Service in which Divine Blessing for the Mayor's year of office, being held at the parish church, as is the custom, it will take place in St Mary's pro-Cathedral at the request of the Mayor-elect, Councillor Eric McMahon, who is a Roman Catholic.'[32]

In 1951, there took place the first Diocesan Synod in the Cathedral, followed by a second one ten years later. A synod is convened to bring to the attention of the clergy matters which directly concern the life and progress of the diocese.[33]

It was during this decade that alterations and extensions were made to the church to accommodate an increasing number of people. A new porch was added in 1952. By the late 1950s, each Sunday there were crowds standing at the back of the church.

> The Pugin church with its arches tended to obscure the view of the High Altar from the side aisles and thus taxed the ingenuity of the architect to bring the congregation into active visual interest in the Mass. 1957 – centenary year – was deemed a propitious time to tackle this problem. Mr F.

C. Roberts, of Mold, the architect, was the person to find the solution. He designed the new altar, planned the new sacristies and porch, together with the alterations to sanctuary and side chapels.'[34]

Mr Eric McMahon.

A new Lady Chapel was incorporated in 1959.[35]

All kinds of ecumenical events have become familiar to us these days and they were given a special impetus by the teaching of Vatican II in the sixties. But they did not begin there. At least as early as 1953, what was then called the Chair of Unity Octave was kept in the cathedral, although the attendance was not large.

Towards the end of the 1950s, the Legion of Mary was founded. The first meeting took place in the Upper Room of St Mary's Hall on 3 June 1957. Its Spiritual Director was Fr. James O'Donoghue and its first President was Brother Mackreth. Members were encouragd to receive Communion frequently and they took part in a variety of good works, including giving support when there were talks for non-Catholics or for the parish mission in January 1959. In September 1959, several members went to Oteley House to do some cleaning in preparation for the nuns [the Little Sisters of the Assumption] coming at the end of the month. In a country with few native vocations to the priesthood, members with children were encouraged to put the idea of the priesthood before them.[36]

> A major part of our experience in the 1950s was the Travelling Mission. This was set up by Bishop Petit, so that Catholics in the more remote areas of the diocese would be able to attend Mass at least from time to time.[37]

In no small part, this was to lead eventually to parishes being established at Overton [1958], Ruabon [1959] and St Anne's, Queen's Park [1962]. Ron Saunders initiated the fundraising for St Anne's at this time. Dr and Mrs McGivern, then living in Lodge, Brymbo were asked to host a Mass organised by Fr. Doyle and other Redemptorist priests based at Machynlleth. Remembered as a genial man, he would visit the area (Brymbo, Pentre Broughton, Southsea) on a Friday, getting in touch with Catholic families and return on Sunday

Canon Evans with members of the choir performing in the local hospital.

Clergy, parishoners and Scouts on the first pilgrimage to Lourdes, 1949.

morning for Confessions and Mass for twenty to thirty people. Later, the Capuchin Friars from Pantasaph carried on the work until the 1960s. Among the priests involved were the then Fr. Aloysius Ward and Fr. Cuthbert Durkin. The former was to become Bishop of Menevia in 1981 and later Archbishop of Cardiff, while the latter became a diocesan priest and now serves St Anne's, Wrexham.[38]

Parishioner Clare Ryan, at this time became an active member of the Catholic Parents and Electors Association and so began her interest in parish affairs.

> It was at a Pastoral Council meeting that the suggestion arose to put Clare forward for the Laity Commission (a national body). She was selected and, attending meetings in London, later acted as Chairperson for several years. Clare loved the work, never missed a meeting and became friendly with many leading people in the Hierarchy and laity of the day. It was at the start of the promotion of ordinary lay Catholics in the affairs of the Church and so had a certain excitement about it. Clare also served on the Commission for Seminaries and, in the diocese, was on the Admission Board for priestly formation. She was a Foundation Governor of St Joseph's School for 30 years, a school very dear to her heart. She was awarded the Pro Ecclesia et Pontifice Medal and was honoured as a Dame of the Holy Sepulchre for her involvement in church work.[39]

The 1960s

Britain in the 1960s was to become known as the home of the 'Swinging Sixties', a decade bringing about a change in attitudes, especially towards sexual morality. The decade of the

Beatles, Mary Quant and the mini-skirt, was to present a challenge to traditional Christianity, especially after the publication of the Pope's encyclical, *Humanae Vitae* in 1968. The Second Vatican Council had been called by Pope John XXIII to bring about *aggiornamento* in the Church. The Bishops of the Church met in Rome from 1963 to 1965 and, eventually this was to bring about a gradual change of attitudes in the way the Church saw itself, essentially, and in relation to the world, other Christian bodies and other religions. Some felt that this would extend to the Church's traditional ban on birth control.

Most obvious to the people in the pew were the further changes in the liturgy, now in English, and sometimes Welsh, with the priest facing the people. Many people were glad, especially converts, who were more at home with a service in their own tongue. Others, though, were unhappy, as they felt that, in losing Latin, they had lost a distinguishing mark of the Church, while some were very unhappy at the re-positioning of the tabernacle.

Fr. Charles Lloyd, a curate at the time, remembers life in St Mary's parish continuing the same as usual. 'Fundraising was the order of the day in order to finance the Catholic schools and the presbytery was almost completely given over to fundraising operations, while the clergy lived in somewhat primitive conditions.'

Funding of their schools placed a very heavy financial burden on Catholics. The system of education was such that state schools and voluntary schools existed side by side. Catholics and other voluntary schools, had to find the money to pay for sites, buildings and structural repairs. Catholics saw themselves as having to pay twice — for their own schools by voluntary contributions and for the state schools through their taxes.

Thus it was that there was regular bingo in the Hall. Ron Saunders from Queen's Park was one of those who organised it. Meanwhile, several pupils from the Convent School, operated as volunteers on Saturday afternoons, counting the money brought in by the football pools.

> The team when I first arrived were Elizabeth Cashman and Francis McMahon. Elizabeth was the niece of Mgr Cashman and her brother, Peter, served on the altar, her parents also being active in the parish. Francis McMahon's father taught at St Joseph's. The second team was Eithne Hughes

Canon Evans, Father Bernard Murphy, Sister Josephine (second from left), Sister Norbert (far right) and First Communicants, 1962.

Bishop Fox (second from left), after being consecrated as Auxilliary Bishop of Menevia, and Bishop Petit (second from right, front row).

and Elizabeth Crowe. Eithne's family were from Ireland and she is now Sister Eithne and working in the Philippines. A former pupil of Holy Family Convent, she and two others from the school, Josie McNay and Mary Hegarty joined the Holy Family Sisters in the late sixties. Josie, who was from Llay, took the name Sr. Cecilia and was Provincial of the Holy Family sisters in the seventies. Mary took the name Sr. Antonia and went to South Africa as a missionary. Elizabeth Crowe's family were 'old' Wrexham. They ran a wholesale fruit and vegetable business.[40]

Activities and organisations in the parish continued and some new ones were added.The choir and the youth club continued. Table tennis proved to be popular and on Sunday evenings, there was dancing. The Knights of St Columba was formed in the sixties and had a junior section, known as the Squires. [41]

By 1964, there was a Union of Catholic Mothers (UCM) in the parish, under the presidency of Mrs Angus and Sr. Josephine, both teachers at St Mary's School, with Mrs Dora Marubbi as its secretary. The meetings always followed Mass. Canon Evans always found time to sit in at the meetings. The UCM members were a great support to the parish priest — they served teas at all parish gatherings in the hall e.g. for all priests and altar servers from all over the diocese on Maundy Thursday and after the Blessed Richard Gwyn procession. This was to become an annual event for many years.

In 1960, several hundreds of people from Denbighshire, Flintshire, Cheshire and Shropshire, including diocesan clergy and nuns processed from the Cathedral to the Beast Market, the scene of his martyrdom in October, 1584. Bishop Petit headed the procession, while Fr. David Lewis, a priest at the Cathedral carried the relic, which had been given to the Bishop by the Jesuits of Manresa College. The special preacher for the afternoon, Fr. James Walsh, SJ, was actively associated with the cause of the Forty Martyrs of England and Wales at the time.[42]

The 1960s were to see a greater commitment to ecumenism, although some clergy found the response of the parishioners of St Mary's disappointing. On 19 January 1965, during the Week of Prayer for Christian Unity, there was a joint denominational meeting at the Memorial Hall, Wrexham addressed by Bishop Petit. Two years later the *Wrexham Leader* reported the Cathedral 'packed for united service', which was the first of its kind to be held in any of the town's churches. The *Leader* went on to say that 'it was an indication of the widespread move towards Christian unity and of the Spirit behind the Ecumenical Movement'.[43]

It was on Low Sunday, 1962, that the new church of St Anne's, Queen's Park was opened. It had cost £30,000 and served about 900 Catholics in the area. They had been served from the pro-Cathedral until now and Mass had been celebrated at the Community Centre by Fr. James O'Donohue, who was now the new parish priest. He was a late vocation and came from Ireland, where he had been a member of the Garda (Police). The parish was later to have its own primary school.[44]

At a diocesan level, under Bishop Petit, a feature of church life in the 1960s and 1970s was the Diocesan Pastoral Council, on which a number of parishioners served. Meetings were held in Wrexham, Machynlleth and Aberystwyth. There was usually a visiting speaker. The topics varied, but there was generally a lively discussion with a good atmosphere.

Thursday, 9 May 1968 was a day of special rejoicing in the Diocese of Menevia. His Lordship Bishop Petit had invited the clergy, religious and laity of his diocese to join with him in the offering of a Solemn Mass of Thanksgiving to mark the Golden Jubilee of his priesthood. The cathedral was crowded to capacity. Outside the cathedral grounds, the pupils of St Mary's Junior School, St Joseph's Secondary School and the Convent High School formed a guard of honour. The Apostolic Delegate, Archbishop Cardinale and fifteen bishops walked in procession into the cathedral, leading the jubilarian to the sanctuary.[45]

The 1970s

By the 1970s, there were 2,680 Roman Catholics living in Wrexham. Canon Evans was still Administrator of the pro-Cathedral, assisted now by three curates, Revs Bernard Lordan, Patrick Murray and Sylvester O'Donnell. The 1970s saw changes at the diocesan level. Bishop Petit celebrated his Silver Jubilee as bishop of the diocese in March 1972. Later the same year, he resigned and on 21 July, Bishop Langton Fox became the sixth bishop of Menevia. He had been Auxiliary Bishop to Bishop Petit since 1965. The following year Bishop Petit died. In November of that year, Bishop Fox gave cause for concern when he was admitted to hospital with jaundice due to a virus infection.

Another sign of greater commitment to inter-church co-operation on the part of the diocese was the two-day Diocesan Conference on Ecumenism held at Aberystwyth on 3 and 4 April, 1970. Delegates attended from all parts of the diocese, including St Mary's Parish, Wrexham. Its stated purpose was to discuss the difficulties and opportunities concerning work for unity among Christians in Menevia. Three papers formed the basis of the conference, providing a very attentive audience with plenty of food for thought and material for discussion. Fr. Leo Caesar, OSB, urged everyone to strive for corporate unity, under the guidance of the Holy Spirit. Dr J. P. Brown, then as now, a parishioner of Holy Cross, Llangollen described the current state of religion in Wales, its decline and the crying need for positive action, while Fr. Bernard Norris urged delegates to look at ecumenism at the local level and ask whether parishes were doing enough. The conference ended with a sense of optimism and a determination to further the efforts of ecumenism in the diocese.[46]

Canon Bernard Morgan remembers the 1970s. He was appointed assistant priest in 1976 and he found the parish very traditional in those days.

> The old regime continued regarding the Parish Priest and his curates. It was no one's fault — just the way things were. Curates did not have much opportunity to take any initiatives. Until this time the most a curate could do was to visit the hospital and do a bit of visiting.

The 11 o'clock Mass on Sunday continued to be in Latin, although not many attended it. Canon Evans was very keen on bingo, which tied up the parish hall four nights each week.

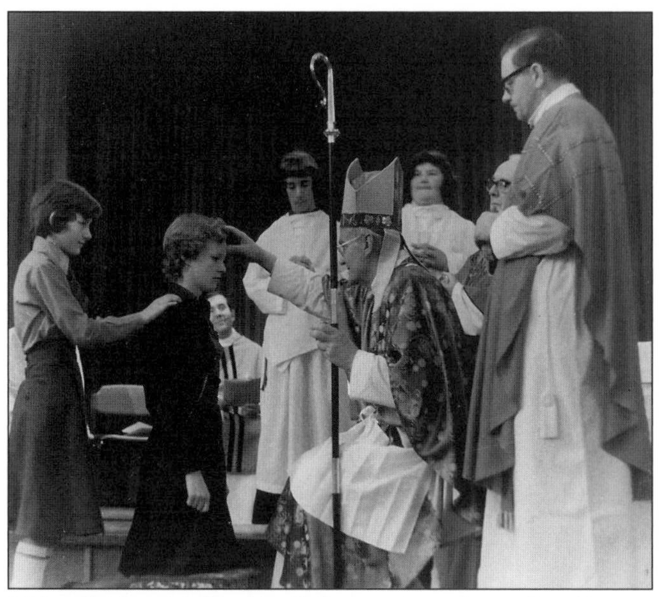

Bishop Petit, assisted by Mgr Kelly, carrying out a confirmation, possibly at St Joseph's School.

Meanwhile, one of the duties of the curates was to drive the school bus; no provision was made by the local authority to transport children to the Catholic schools. Fr. Lordan, a fellow curate with Canon Morgan, had to take the bus to the outlying areas to pick up children for school and take them back at the end of the school day. So he drove the bus each day and spent four nights each week at bingo.

Fr. Lordan's transfer to another parish provided something of a breakthrough in the liturgy. Until this time traditional hymns were the order of the day, but for his going away Mass, Fr. Morgan and Sr. Clare, the sacristan, arranged a Mass, using modern hymns, which fitted in exactly with what was happening. Soon, a Folk Mass was started in the parish. It was important to get the basics right in the parish, and the prayer-life of the parish was seen as of prime importance. A Charismatic Prayer Group began meeting in the Upper Room. This was to lead to all sorts of changes, including the setting-up of a bereavement group, to help people at a very vulnerable time in their lives.[47] The organisations such as the SVP still flourished; the Legion of Mary was strong with both Senior and Junior Praesidia.

The world was continuing to change, and the pace of change was accelerating. This affected all areas of life, but in the parish, it was most evident in marriage and family life. Marriage was going through a difficult time and ways were sought to help the situation. There was a noticeable change in the family problems compared with even twenty years previously. New steps needed to be taken to address these problems and to help people. So, at about this time, Fr. Morgan introduced Marriage Encounter into the parish, to support and strengthen marriages. About seven or eight couples did a Marriage Encounter weekend, coming back into the parish, enthused by their deepened relationships. This was to lead to a parish programme, culminating in the various organisations having a special Mass. Senior citizens were encouraged to share the history of the parish and from these meetings came the idea of a parish yearbook in 1977–8.

A pre-marriage course was started, while the clergy continued to work with people on a personal level. Later, the Association for Separated and Divorced Catholics was formed to help people finding themselves in a particularly difficult situation.[48]

The 1980s

The opening of the 1980s saw the eagerly-awaited National Pastoral Congress. Held in Liverpool in May 1980, its objective was the renewing of the spiritual life and mission of the Catholic Church in Britain. Delegates from all parts of Britain took part including those from Wrexham. An even greater event in the life of the church was the visit of Pope John Paul II to Britain in May 1982. Over 1,000 people from the Wrexham area made their way by coach to Cardiff to attend the Papal Mass in Pontcanna Fields. A visible reminder of that event can be seen in the Cathedral — the lectern used by the Holy Father on that occasion.

Canon Schwarz baptising one of the Sznerch children in the 1980s.

During the 1980s, there were changes at both diocesan and parish level. On 1 October 1980, Fr. John Aloysius Ward, OFM Cap, a Franciscan, was consecrated by Bishop Fox, to be his Auxiliary Bishop succeeding him as Bishop of Menevia on 5 February 1981. He, in turn, was succeeded by Bishop James Hannigan, when he moved to Cardiff as Archbishop. Bishop Hannigan was consecrated by him as the eighth bishop of Menevia on 21 November 1983. It was during his episcopate that what had been the two dioceses of Cardiff and Menevia were formed into the three dioceses of Cardiff, Menevia and Wrexham. The new diocese, centred on Swansea retained the title of Menevia, while the northernmost diocese became the diocese of Wrexham. The new diocese of Wrexham was established by a decree of Pope John Paul II on 18 March 1987 and Bishop Hannigan was translated to Wrexham on 12 February 1987.

Meanwhile, at parish level, Canon Adolph Evans, the much-loved Administrator of the Cathedral since 1947 died on 15 April 1982 and his place was taken by Canon Cyril Schwarz, who had been a curate at the cathedral some years before. Iain Cameron, a long-time member of St Mary's parish was ordained to the permanent diaconate by Bishop Ward on 1 November 1981. Common in the early church, the diaconate, a sacrament of service, was restored as a proper and permanent rank of the hierarchy following the Second Vatican Council. Rev. Iain Cameron was the fourth man to be ordained permanent deacon in the old diocese of Menevia. By the early 1980s, Mass attendance at the Cathedral was 1,073 on a Sunday. The parish was developing. While the established organisations continued, there were also new activities for parishioners to take part in. In all, over 160 people were members of these, as well as participating in many events as they took

Lourdes HCPT (Group 155) Wrexham, Handicapped Children's Pilgrimage Trust.

Visit of Pope John Paul II to Cardiff, 1982. Members of the Wrexham group at Pontcanna Fields.

place in the parish. One of the new organisations was 'Choice', aimed at the eighteen–thirty-five age group. Then there was 'Family Friends', the Folk Mass group, 'Marriage Encounter'to support marriages, the Prayer Group, Popmobility and Old Time Dancing — in fact something for all tastes.[49]

Fr. Terry Carr, coming to the cathedral as a curate in 1986 remembers that:

> ... at the cathedral at the time a great deal was happening and there was a tremendous amount of energy and goodwill and activity among the young families of the parish. We had a very active Liturgy Committee as well as many other organisations, which contributed a considerable amount to the life of the parish and there always seemed to be someone to do something; it was a good time to be at the cathedral. I enjoyed that aspect of it enormously. The groups which I tended to take part in were the HCPT (the Handicapped Childrens Pilgrimage Trust) and the Liturgy Committee, a subject which interests me greatly. We did some para-liturgical services in the cathedral during that time, enjoyed greatly by the people of the parish. One of the things which Fr. Morrin and I tried to do was to set up a proper programme of preparation of parents for the baptism of their children and also for First Reconciliation, Holy Communion and Confirmation. These met with limited success. We also set up the Catholic Marriage Advisory Council (CMAC now Marriage Care) in the parish under the auspices of Bishop Hannigan and run by Richard and Yvonne Whitaker and Iain and Vicki Cameron. We also drew up a Marriage Preparation course which was successful at the time. Our main concern was to balance new initiatives with the more traditional organisations.

Now joined by fellow-curate Fr. Adrian Wilcock, Fr. Carr experienced a very difficult period during Canon Schwarz's illness, when he became a senior curate with only a few years experience, temporarily in charge of the Cathedral and immersed in administration. Nevertheless, Fr. Carr found his time at the cathedral both a challenging and an enjoyable experience.[50]

The end of the decade saw a sad day for the Cathedral parish and the diocese of Wrexham, when people heard the news of Mrs Clare Ryan's sudden death on 19 July 1988. She had worked untiringly at parish, diocesan and national level, receiving the Pro Ecclesia et Pontifice Award and becoming a Dame of the Holy Sepulchre in 1982. Together with the death of Canon Schwarz in the following year, this was the end of an era.

The 1990s

By 1990 there were on average 1,177 attending mass each Sunday. Again, the decade was to experience many changes at both parish and diocesan level. Bishop Hannigan died 6 March 1994, to be succeeded by Bishop Edwin Regan on 13 December of the same year.

In the parish, Canon Schwarz was succeeded by Fr. Bernard Morgan in 1989, having spent a short time as Acting Administrator during the last year of Canon Schwarz's life. He had a brain tumour and his faculties were weakening all the time, especially his memory. Canon Morgan recalls that 'He was a legend in his own time, with all the work he did for the diocese.' With Frs. Adrian Wilcock, Stephen Marsh and Aelred (George) McLloughlin as his curates and Deacon Iain Cameron, Canon Bernard Morgan spent ten years at the cathedral as Administrator. Amid great rejoicing, a new church, the Holy Family, was opened in Coedpoeth, replacing the one serving that area since 1949.

During this time, there were a number of new initiatives. Programmes were set up for Readers and Eucharistic Ministers and Fr. Adrian Wilcock was made responsible for the music at the Cathedral. New music was introduced and as well as a senior choir, there was also a junior choir. The Rite of Christian Initiation [RCIA] was started at this time.

> It was a tremendous boost, receiving about 60 people into the Church over the years. People were no longer received into the Church in secrecy. Now, everything was done in a parish context. At every stage people knew about it. It all culminated in a lovely liturgy, when people were received at the Easter ceremonies.[51]

A Hospitality Group was formed to serve refreshments in St Mary's Hall at all kinds of functions and occasions, and a Cafod Group was formed with its aim to encourage local people to offer spiritual and practical assistance to their fellow human beings in developing countries. A Friday Self-Denial Scheme was introduced. To help with marriages, as well as Marriage Care, Dr Pat Walters, with a qualified team offered instruction to couples on Natural Family Planning. Guided Prayer was offered by the St Beuno's Outreach team at about this time.

In the wider world of Wrexham, since 1990, the parish had been a full member of *Cytun* — the title of the former Council of Churches and has sought, in accordance with the Gospel 'that all may be one.' Members of all the churches pray together in friendship and share a common concern for local social issues such as homelessness. Catholics have served on the executive and continue to have a responsibility for the development of church unity in Wrexham. St Mary's was the first Catholic parish to join TCC (*Trefnu Cymunedol Cymru* / Together Creating Community). Its purpose is broad-based organising — a practical method of bringing together churches and many other groups to campaign on issues of common concern, with the intention of effecting change and advancing the interests of ordinary people, especially the poor and the powerless.

In 1994, Pope John Paul II published an encyclical, *Tertio Milennio Adveniente* in preparation for the Millenium, the year 2000, when the church would be challenged to promote the mission of Christ in the economic, social, political and cultural affairs of our time. 1997-9 was a preparation for this. 1997 focussed on Jesus Christ, the Word of God; 1998 focussed on the Holy Spirit and his sanctifying presence, while 1999 focussed on God the Father.

In 1997, the Bishops 'Conference of England and Wales' produced a document entitled *The Common Good*. In the time before the General Election, it spoke to the whole nation. 'In our own parish the political candidates were each sent a copy. They came to our parish to listen to our concerns in this context and to offer their responses.'[52]

Stimulated by the hopes and expectations expressed by the Holy Father, the parish was invited to take part in planning its direction beyond the year 2000. Parishioners were encouraged to reflect on the different dimensions of Christian life in the parish. The aim was

Papal Nuncio visiting St Joseph's School, 2006.

to develop a greater richness as a Christian community, allowing Gospel values to be seen as active in parish life and to have new meaning and vibrancy for succes-sive generations.

In early 1998, an exhibition celebrating the parish was mounted and everyone was invited to share their personal and community involvement in parish life, past and present. There were two parish Open Meetings when people expressed their hopes and expectations for the future and during Advent, the Bishop led reflections on the meaning and celebration of the Eucharist. One of the results of the St Mary's Beyond 2000 initiative was the creation of the Parish Advisory Council, bringing together parishioners who volunteered or were nominated by others, together with priests, deacons and school representatives to meet and discuss issues of importance in the parish. The constitution of the Council begins with a dedication — in the spirit of Our Lady, the patron of the parish — to become a collaborative Parish Community.

An article in the *Parish Yearbook* for 1999 states:

> We live in an age when the Second Vatican Council has shifted the focus from a Church which was embattled and apart to a Church that is in the world and for the world; slowly but surely we are beginning to accept that God is calling us to function in a wider sphere. The infant Church followed this pattern and so must we.

Quoting the report *The Sign We Give*, published by the Bishops' Conference, the article concluded, 'We are convinced that the manner and style of relationships in the Church is part of the sign it gives and for this reason we must develop patterns of collaborative ministry, not simply to renew the life of the Church, but to enable the Church to be part of transforming the world.'[53]

In February 1999, Canon Morgan departed for pastures new in Bangor, while Bangor's parish priest, Fr. Peter Brignall came to replace him at the Cathedral. In all, Canon Morgan had spent sixteen years in Wrexham. Since Fr. Brignall came to the Cathedral in 1999, a momentous event was a fitting celebration of the Millennium, 2000 years since the birth of Jesus Christ. A Millennium Service marked the event, while, as part of the celebrations, an icon commemorating St Richard Gwyn was commissioned. It was crafted by Sr. Petra Clare, a Benedictine nun and blessed on Sunday, 16 October 2000 by Bishop Edwin Regan.

The first decade of the new Millenium has brought an influx of Catholics from various parts of the world into the parish, each nationality coming with their own gifts and cultures. These include Catholics from Poland, Portugal, the Philippines and Kerala in India, all enriching the life of the parish in their own particular way.

Recently, Wrexham has had another Catholic Mayor in George James (2006–07). He was born in Brecon on 3 January 1949 and moved to Wrexham as a child. He attended both St

Canon Morgan and a group of First Communicants, 1990s.

Father Brignall and a group of First Communicants, 2006.

George James, Mayor of Wrexham.
[Wrexham County Borough Council]

Mary's and St Joseph's Schools before studying at Plater College, Oxford. He then worked for the Gas Board. Starting as a community councillor, he went on to serve Wrexham Borough and Wrexham County Borough Council in all for twenty years. His concerns have been planning, housing, children and young people, youth services and education. He qualified as a youth leader and at one time worked at Queen's Park in that capacity. He had been the first altar server in St Anne's Church. During his term as mayor, he has been accompanied by his daughter, the Mayoress Mrs Victoria Barlow, who was also a past pupil of St Joseph's school. Now well into the twenty-first century, the main focus will be the celebrations surrounding the 150th anniversary of the building of St Mary's.

And so the story of the Catholics in Wrexham moves on. Carrying the memory of the parishioners who have gone before us, who served the Lord faithfully in their own time, we are called to face the challenges of the Third Millenium with similar faithfulness in a manner suited to our own time.

References

1. *Catholic Directory*, 1905.
2. Wrexham Diocesan Archives, Quinn MS, 1903.
3. *Wrexham Advertiser*, 8 September 1914.
4. Frank More's Memoirs.
5. SVP Secretary's Report, 1927.
6. Frank More's Memoirs.
7. *Wrexham Advertiser*, 5 October 1934.
8. Wrexham Diocesan Archives.
9. SVP Secretary's Report, 1933.
10. Wrexham Diocesan Archives.
11. Programme Cathedral Archives.
12. Frank More's Memoirs.
13. Wrexham Diocesan Archives.
14. Wrexham Diocesan Archives.
15. Wrexham Diocesan Archives.
16. Frank More's Memoirs.
17. Wrexham Diocesan Archives.
18. Cathedral Archives.
19. Wrexham Diocesan Archives.
20. Wrexham Diocesan archives.
21. Cathedral Archives.
22. *Menevia Record*.
23. Information supplied by Mrs Irena Szenderowicz.
24. Information supplied by Mrs Rosanna Jones.
25. Diocesan Archives.
26. *Menevia Record*, 1948.
27. Wrexham Diocesan Archives.
28. Information supplied by Paul Elson.

29. *Wrexham Leader*, 9 September 1949.
30. Information supplied by Paul Elson.
31. Frank More's Memoirs.
32. *Wrexham Leader*, 25 April 1952.
33. Wrexham Diocesan Archives.
34. *Menevia Record*, 1947.
35. Wrexham Diocesan archives.
36. Legion of Mary Minute Book.
37. Frank More's Memoirs.
38. Information supplied by Esther McGivern.
39. Information supplied by Esther McGivern.
40. Information supplied by Father Charles Lloyd and Sister Eithne Hughes.
41. Wrexham Diocesan Archives.
42. *Menevia Record*, December, 1960.
43. *Wrexham Leader*, 24 January 1967.
44. *Menevia Record*, September 1962.
45. *Menevia Record*, 1968.
46. Wrexham Diocesan Archives.
47. Canon Bernard Morgan's Reminiscences.
48. Canon Bernard Morgan's Reminiscences.
49. Canon Bernard Morgan's Reminiscences.
50. Father Terry Carr's Reminiscences.
51. Canon Bernard Morgan's Reminiscences.
52. Sister Sheila O'Hara, LSU.
53. Keith McDonogh and Sister Sheila O'Hara, LSU.

CHAPTER SEVEN

The Sisters

During almost 130 years since the first group of nuns arrived in Wrexham, a large number have followed them, all making a valuable contribution to Catholic life and worship in the town. Altogether there have been six convents established here and, although most of the nuns have been Irish, their orders were originally founded in France or had a French connection.

The Holy Family Sisters – also known as Sisters of the Immaculate Conception

The Holy Family Sisters were the first nuns to come to Wrexham and a number of them remain in the town until this day. Over the years, they have performed great service in all three of Wrexham's Catholic schools as well as taking part in all kinds of activities in the parish

Their order's founder, Father Pierre Bienvenue Noailles, had set up the Institute of the Holy Family of Bordeaux in 1820 in the aftermath of the French Revolution. The aim was to strengthen people's faith and witness in the hope that Christian values would permeate throughout society.[1]

Their connection with Wrexham began in 1879. The Very Reverend Provost Hilton, Missionary Rector of Wrexham, wanting some nuns to teach in the school, wrote to the sisters at Rockferry, Wirral, begging them to take charge of the Mixed and Infants School in Brook Street. Four of them took up their duties on 1 March 1879.[2]

The Catholic population of Wrexham appreciated the coming of the Sisters, who immediately began their apostolic work, both with the children in the parochial school and among the sick and poor of the parish. At first they lived at 22 Regent Street, near the Infirmary, where, by 1889, they were receiving a 'limited number of young ladies for private lessons in Music, Painting, Drawing, Singing and Modern Languages' at their Convent High School on the premises.[3]

By 1891, there were seven sisters living there, four of them having been born in Ireland. Their Superior was Sr. St John, aged thirty-four. Other sisters were Sisters Ursula, Margaret Mary, Mary Nativity, Anastasia, Angelica and Bonaventure.[4]

In the early years of the twentieth century, the sisters developed a musical tradition in St Mary's Schools and the children took part in annual operatic performances at the Drill Hall in the town to very large audiences.[5]

As their work developed in Wrexham, the community increased in numbers and they needed a new home. With Bishop Mostyn's assistance, a house in Grosvenor Road was obtained, which was to become the Convent Grammar School. Meanwhile, the Sisters continued to be in charge of the Primary and Infants' Schools.

By the time of Bishop Hannan's visitation on 21 March 1942, there were twenty-six sisters living in the Convent of the Immaculate Conception, Grosvenor Road. Apart from their duties in the Convent and the schools, some of the Sisters were involved in parish activities. Among the sisters at that time were:

> Rev Mother Clotilde, Superioress
> Sr. Angelica, Head Mistress, Convent School
> Sr. Trea, Head Mistress, St Mary's Junior
> Sr. Aquinas, Head Mistress, St Mary's Infants
> Sr. Oswald, Music Mistress
> Sr. Pauline, Class Mistress, St Mary's. She also instructed converts and was a member of the Children of Mary
> Sr. Rita, Class Mistress at St Mary's, Sacristan and member of the Altar Society [6]

Sister Cecilia McNay, Provincial of Holy Family Sisters, 1970s.

After the closing of the Convent School in 1972, the property in Grosvenor Road was too large for the Sisters, so in 1974 they moved to their present home, Plas Derwen, Sontley Road, where, now retired from active work, a number still live. Another of their number, Sr. Elizabeth, is housekeeper at Bishop's House across the road. In their retirement, they have been involved in the SVP, Scripture groups, prayer groups, voluntary work and with the Associates, a group of women sharing in the charism of the sisters, modelling their Christian lives on the life of the Holy Family of Nazareth.

For over 130 years the Holy Family Sisters have made an outstanding contribution to education in Wrexham through the Convent Grammar School and St Mary's Primary School in the spirit of their founder.

Sisters of St Joseph of the Apparition

It was to be over sixty years before another order joined the Holy Family Sisters in Wrexham. The Sisters of St Joseph of the Apparition took up residence in Plas Derwen, Sontley Road on 25 August 1943, at the request of Bishop Hannan. Their new home belonged to the Bishop and had been built in the 1860s for John Beirne, a

Draft Agreement
between
Wrexham Mission and the Sisters of the I. Concepn

1. The Sisters undertake all the teaching in the Elementary Schools subject of course to the Priest in charge of the Mission.
2. That they help generally in the work of the Missi under the direction of the Priest:
3. In consideration for teaching in the Schools they shall receive at least £70 a year for each Certificated Sister and at least £40 for each Assistant Sister. The number of such teaching Sisters not to be less than 2 Certificated and 2 Assistants Art. 68
4. The Sisters have the right to carry on a Private High School
5. That no salary shall be expected by the Priest in charge for Chaplain's work unless the Establishment is notably increased.
6. Mass at least once a week and Confessions of Nuns to be heard in the Convent.

Sarah Morrin
M. C. Delaney
J. Gelleburt
Sup. Gen.

+ Francis Bp. of Ascalon
V. A. of Wales

Draft agreement between Wrexham Mission and the Holy Family Sisters, 1898. [Wrexham Diocesan Archives]

Canon Evans with a group of First Communicants, 1961.

prominent Catholic in the town and its Mayor in 1876.

The Bishop was anxious to establish a nursing home in Wrexham and in response to his appeal to the sisters at Whalley Range, Manchester, three sisters were sent to begin the work in the difficult circumstances of wartime. Much needed to be done to make it ready for use as a nursing home. In all, eight sisters led a quiet, simple, but hard life in the service of the suffering.[7]

The order had been founded in the mid-nineteenth century by Emilie de Vialar, a noble Frenchwoman, who spent her life in works of charity to the sick, poor and suffering. She was canonized in 1951. In the spirit of their foundress, it was the special hope and prayer of her sisters in Wrexham, that they might, by their work and example pass on the Good News of the love of God for mankind.[8] Because of financial problems within the order, the sisters had to close down the nursing home and they left Wrexham.

Little Sisters of the Assumption

It was on the feast of St Michael, the Archangel, in September 1958, that the Little Sisters of the Assumption opened their new convent at Oteley House, Salisbury Road, at the request of Bishop Petit.[9]

The congregation had been founded in France in 1865, by Fr. Etienne Pernet, an Augustinian of the Assumption, who while professor in Nimes, was afforded a close-up view of the great misery of the working-class people as a result of industrialisation in the nineteenth century. His nuns were to support these people in their own homes in any way necessary, nursing the sick, looking after the children, cooking and cleaning, thus loving and serving Christ in the poor.

On their arrival in Wrexham, the people of the parish, especially members of the Legion of Mary, soon rallied round to help the sisters in a practical way, with painting and decorating, clearing the ground and forming a garden and cementing the yard.[10] Before long, two sisters began nursing training at the Maelor General Hospital and were soon accepted there. Day-by-day, the sisters became a familiar sight going about their works of mercy. By the 1960s, people became used to seeing them getting about the town on their motor scooters.

The first group of Little Sisters with Bishop Petit, 1958.

A Little Sister visiting a family.

The first Superior was Sr. Brigid Keane, the following making up the founding community — Sr. Mary Donnelly, Sr. Agnes Quirke, Sr. Teresa O'Neill, Sr. Sheila Fennessy and Sr. Esther O'Neill.

The Little Sisters nursed well over 1,500 patients in their time, the chronic sick, young mothers with acute illness and terminal cases of cancer of all ages. The majority of their patients were Church-in-Wales, Baptists , Presbyterians and Methodists and in their own quiet way, the Little Sisters were able to forge a bond of unity with all denominations and had respect and co-operation from all of their ministers. But eventually due to a lack of vocations, the order had to close down Oteley House in 1998 and most of the sisters returned to Ireland, where they had come from. Sr. Esther is now the only Little Sister remaining in Wrexham.[11]

Sisters of St Joseph of Chambery

In July 1960, Bishop Petit asked that Sisters of St Joseph of Chambery be assigned to house-keeping duties at Bishop's House in Wrexham for him, his two elderly sisters and two priest-secretaries.

The order had its roots in France. It was during the seventeenth century, in the town of Le Puy, in France, that Fr. Jean-Pierre Medaille brought together a group of women from which the congregation grew. As a missionary, he came into contact with many young girls and widows, who, touched by the misery wrought by civil and religious warfare, wanted to give themselves to the Lord and to try to reach out to the suffering around them. Under his direction, these women met spontaneously in little groups to help one another in their quest for God and to help relieve the misery all around them. From such small beginnings grew the congregation of the Sisters of St Joseph of Chambery. In response to the call of the church, the sisters departed for distant countries, including India in 1851. By the 1930s, the mission in India had declined, so that two Irish sisters journeyed to Ireland, in search of young women interested in the religious life. Events overtook them when war broke out and, being unable to return to India, it was suggested that they come to Wales and eventually, Wrexham. In Wrexham, the Sisters lived and worked at Bishop's House until Bishop Petit retired in 1972. They then moved to rented accommodation in Salisbury Road for a year before moving to what is their present convent in Derby Road.

For several years, some sisters worked in the three Catholic schools in Wrexham, while others trained and worked as nurses. They also contributed to the life of the parish, Sr. Maureen being choir-mistress for many years. At present, Sr. Maureen remains at the Derby Road convent with Sister Catherine.[12]

The Poor Sisters of Nazareth

It was Bishop Petit again who encouraged the Poor Sisters of Nazareth to come to Wrexham and develop a residential old-folks home alongside a mother-and-baby home. In 1963, Hillbury House, near to Bishop's House, came on the market and long seeing the need in Wrexham for the work which this order undertook, Bishop Petit visualized this property as a possible centre for the work. Describing it as 'a very lovely property indeed'[13] he blessed and officially opened the new foundation on 21 December 1966. He spoke of the Christian work of the Sisters of Nazareth and of their devoted care of all.

The Congregation of the Poor Sisters of Nazareth was founded in 1851 by Victoire Larmenier, a young French girl, at the request of Cardinal Wiseman. The first house was established at Brook Green, London. Finding their inspiration in the Holy Family of Nazareth, the special aim of the Congregation has been the care of the aged, whom they receive into their houses, and the care of needy and abandoned children. The Sisters have also established maternity homes for unmarried mothers.[14]

In Wrexham, many an old person was happy to end their days in the care of the sisters, while in the mother-and-baby home, hundreds of babies were delivered, especially by Sr. Celine who always had Dr Toby Ryan on hand should the need arise. The local newspaper remarked on the serene and happy atmosphere at Nazareth House, which was up-to-date in every way.[15] The Sisters were eager to help and serve. Theirs was a dedicated life, hidden and humble, and at times, wearing. Due to shortage of vocations, in recent years the Sisters have had to withdraw from Wrexham. Nazareth House, now retaining its original name, Hillbury Care Home, remains a residential home for the elderly.

La Sainte Union Sisters

The Sisters of La Sainte Union have been in Wrexham since 1987, living at the Peace and Justice Centre, 35–7 Kingsmills Road. Father Owen Hardwicke, who founded the Centre in the 1980s, is still engaged with its concerns and his commitment to non-violence issues is nationally and internationally well-known. The Sisters are engaged with a wide range of peace and justice issues.

They began by establishing a base in the diocese for the work of Cafod, the national Catholic Agency for Overseas Development. This work is now led by a paid organiser, Mrs Katja Jewell and continues to operate from the Peace ad Justice Centre. The Sisters are also involved, either directly or indirectly with TCC (*Trefnu Cymunedol Cymru* or Together Creating Communities). TCC is a broad-based coalition of diverse faith and community groups working together to improve conditions in their localities. The organisation has dealt competently with issues such as policing, noise, youth, environment, waste disposal, living-wage concepts, homelessness etc. In the process, local people have learned how to deal with politicians, industry, councils, unions and the voluntary sector.

Accommodation is offered at the Centre for a number of groups dealing with issues related to justice and peace, e. g. in some areas with involvement by the Sisters — Local Peace and Justice Committee, the Diocesan Child Protection Committee, Parish meetings and Cytun Lenten Church-Unity Prayer Group. Library facilities are available for people wishing to study religious and social themes in a limited number of areas. Individual commitment of the five LSU Sisters attached to the Centre include Parish Choir, Parish Hospitality, Parish Meetings, School Governor Representation, Senior School Chaplaincy, Church-Unity weekly prayer meetings, support for a local 'Save the Family' concern, a modest contact with asylum seekers, mostly through Salvation Army contacts. They are also responsible for the administration (Finance, Maintenance and Management) of a fairly busy Centre. Networking in all areas has borne a rich reward. This is especially true of Cafod and TCC.

The founder of the order, Jean Baptiste Debrabant (1801–80), as a young priest in the Archdiocese of Cambrai, France, was challenged by the needs of his time. Recognising the gifts and potential of a group of dedicated women in his parish, he founded in 1825, the Congregation of La Sainte Union, which through Christian education would be able to bring the Gospel message to a de-Christianised society in post-Revolutionary France. The Sisters have tried to respond, as far as they have been able, to the needs locally, nationally and globally in the twenty-first century. 'Our call is to be at the heart of the world, revealing God's love'.[16]

References

1. *Menevia Record*, November 1957.
2. SLAUGHTER, Mgr Edward,*History of the diocese of Shrewsbury*, p41.
3. *Wrexham Advertiser*, 10 August 1889.
4. 1891 Census.
5. *Wrexham Advertiser*, 23 March 1907.
6. Wrexham Diocesan Archives Visitation, 1942.
7. Wrexham Diocesan Archives, letter from Sr. Judith, Superior n.d.
8. *Menevia Record*, August 1954 .
9. Ibid, September 1961.
10. Legion of Mary Minutes.
11. Diocesan Directory, 1997.
12. 'Sisters of St Joseph of Chambery' and 'Our history in Wales from 1939' by the Sisters and from information supplied by Sister Maureen.
13. Wrexham Diocesan Archives: letter from Bishop Petit to Mother General, 22 September 1963.
14. *Menevia Record*, 1967.
15. *Wrexham Advertiser*.
16. Article 1, La Sainte Union Constitutions, 1984, and from information supplied by Sister Sheila O'Hara, LSU.

CHAPTER EIGHT

The Schools

St Mary's Primary School

St Mary's Roman Catholic Primary School is now situated in Lea Road, Wrexham. Its motto is '*Credu, Gobeitho, Caru*' (Faith, Hope, Love) and it includes David Lord, VC, among its former pupils.

The story of St Mary's Primary School has been, above all, one of change. It was not always known as St Mary's and it was not always known as a primary school. Until the opening of St Joseph's in 1960, it was an all-age school. But, more significantly than changing its character, it has changed its location no less than twelve times.

The Roman Catholic Church has always placed a high value on education and in 1840, in the time of Fr. John Tobin, the first Roman Catholic 'poor school' was set up in a room in St David's Chapel, King Street catering for about fifty children — perhaps that is why an extension was made to the building during that year. At the time, there were about half-a-dozen schools in Wrexham. It was one of four Roman Catholic schools in Wales and the only one in north Wales.[1]

By 1850, the school was over a blacksmith's shop in Yorke Street. By September 1851, the school was in Bank Street and the *Wrexham Advertiser* for 1 October 1851 announced:

> Roman Catholic Day Schools Public Examination — a school under the direction of the Roman Catholics of this town has been established some 12–15 months in Bank St, Wrexham. On Thursday the 18th inst a public examination of the boys in the various branches taught in the school took place. The general acquirements by the boys were very creditable to the master, especially when it is remembered the short time the school has been in operation. In history, geography, grammar and arithmetic the boys seemed proficient, some of them evincing considerable abilities. Much praise is due to the Rev. Mr Havard for the great interest he has taken in the success of the school and for his unremitting exertions to secure it.[2]

By 1852, it was being held in a room over the Temperance House in Bank Street, which much later was to become Marubbi's Café. 'The school was small, numbering only fifty pupils. The schoolmaster was Mr Tierney, who lived in King Street with the priest, at that time — Fr. John Coulstone'.[3] Two years later, it was removed to a room belonging to Mr McDermott, situated at the rear of Mr Stokes' paint shop in Yorke Street. The numbers then had risen to sixty, and the scholars were taught by Mr Cassidy. The priest at the time was Fr. John Reah, Canon of Shrewsbury.

The Temperance House in Bank Street, site of the school in 1852.

In 1856 it had returned to Bank Street, but not to the original premises. It was held in a room over the shop of Mr Owen, confectioner, etc at the bottom of the street. It seems to have remained there only one year, for in 1857 it had taken up its quarters in the Priest's House in King Street. The mistress was a Miss Law.[4]

Another move became necessary in 1860, possibly due to the increase in numbers; there were between seventy and eighty pupils by now. Mrs Parfitt and her daughter, both uncertificated teachers, ran the school in a room over a coach-building factory in Hill Street. Mrs Parfitt's son, a postman, was to be the organist at St Mary's Church many years later.

Then, the school closed for a time, re-opening in February 1867. The teacher is said to have been a certificated Christian Brother by the name of Mr George Riack. When the school was visited by the Very Rev. D. Browne and Mr Byrne, a contributor to the school fund, they found the attendance scanty, many parents being unaware that the school had reopened. In the same year, there was a mission in the parish conducted by the Redemptorists, with a special mission for children.[5]

The first Government report on the school was in June 1868 and found the school hopelessly overcrowded.

> [It] ... could hardly contain one-half of the annual average which has been placed into it. The managers, sensible of the impossibility of this continuing with government aid, have, I am glad to say, already taken the preliminary steps towards building a suitable schoolroom by making arrangements for the purchase of land. But as the erection of a building will occupy a considerable time, they are advised to endeavour, without delay, to obtain one large room or two rooms into which the school could be removed, and properly accommodated, during the building of the new school-house.

A government grant was allowed, only on condition that more suitable premises were found while the new school was being built, the present room being only sufficient for thirty-eight children. Mr Riack had remained only about a year and resigned the post in July 1868, to be succeeded by Miss Elizabeth Christian.[6]

The adverse government report made it impossible to remain in the premises in Hill Street and John Beirne, always a great benefactor to the school offered to house the children in Mount House.

The following summer, while the school was at Mount House, the children,

> ... enjoyed a happy holiday at the Glascoed, the residence of Mrs John Lynch, by whose kind invitation a large number of day scholars belonging to the ... school (140) were assembled and conveyed in carts (provided by Mr McDermott of Mount St) to the beautiful and romantic scenery of the amphitheatre of hills in which Glascoed is nestled. The length of the journey and

the oppressive heat of a glorious harvest day were both forgotten ... by the frequent song and hearty cheers of the little ones. Mrs Lynch and her little daughters welcomed them and conducted by them to a shady & grassy seat in front of the Glascoed. Here, arranged in four lines they were refreshed with excellent lemonade and buns and then dismissed for recreation.

Some boys played cricket , while a large number walked in the woods where the nut trees had irresistible attractions ... After enthusiastically expressing their gratitude ... they returned home, reaching Wxm at 9 o'clock and waking up the good old town with ringing cheers and shouts of gladness ... Dr Browne accompanied the excursion and did his utmost to promote the enjoyment of all. He was ably seconded by Miss Christian {the mistress of the school}. The children were much indebted to to the donor of the tea for such an enjoyable day.[7]

Before long, a piece of land was purchased by Dr Browne 'who has greatly exerted himself in this matter'[8] and a purpose-built school erected on the corner of Brook Street and Vicarage Hill. The stone-laying ceremony was performed by Mrs Watkin Williams, wife of the MP for the Borough. Charles Dodd remembered an 'imposing array of ecclesiastics, including the Very Rev. Dr Browne, the Missionary Rector of Wrexham, Canons Chapman, Buquet and Frith and the Revs Coulstone, Slaughter and O'Brian. Addresses appropriate to the occasion were delivered by Mr Watkin Williams and Dr Browne.'[9] The site and cottages cost £150 and the school was built at the low cost of £550, as the site was cleared by voluntary labour.[10]

The Brook Street School opened on 11 April 1870,

The children assembled in church at 8.30. After Mass they marched in procession to the new school headed by Dr Browne, who blessed the school. Songs and hymns were then sung by the children for the visitors.

Two weeks later, the government inspection report described the new building as:

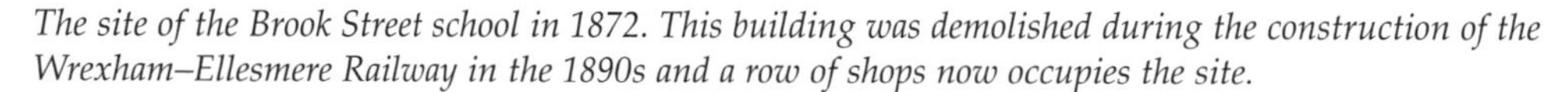

The site of the Brook Street school in 1872. This building was demolished during the construction of the Wrexham–Ellesmere Railway in the 1890s and a row of shops now occupies the site.

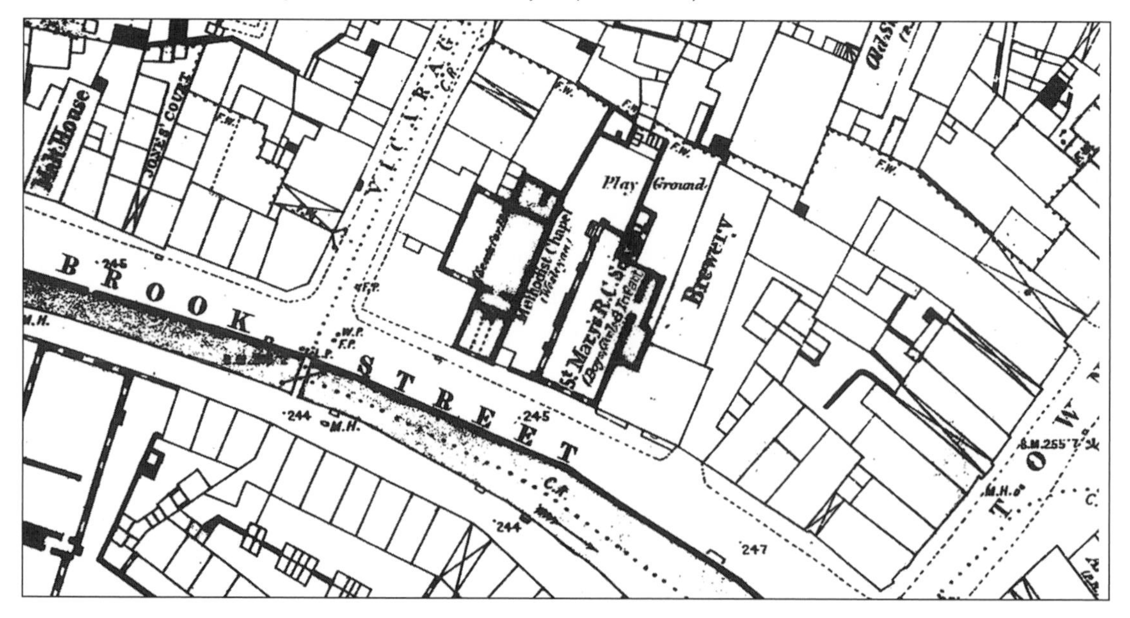

> … an excellent school house, well-ventilated and lighted, of ample dimensions, fully equipped internally and occupying a central position in Wrexham … A zealous and competent mistress conducts the education of the children who attend it and deserves much credit for the efficiency which pervades their discipline and instruction.[11]

The number on the school register was 190 by the 1871 inspection on 17 June, with an average attendance of 120. Next day, prizes for good conduct and attendance were distributed, Catherine Mulligan of Standard IV heading the list.[12]

The school continued to grow. An 1874 diocesan report on its schools reveals that there were 248 children on the books, while the average attendance was 113. Discipline was excellent, but the children were weak in prayers and religious instruction.[13] Miss Christian remained until 1877, apart from an interval of just over a year from May 1871 to September 1872, during which time Miss Kay took over. A Miss McCormack succeeded Miss Christian, staying until the arrival of the Sisters from Rockferry in 1879. Sr. St John became headmistress of the school, with three other sisters helping her.[14]

The school building had been in use for twenty years when in 1890, the Wrexham & Ellesmere Railway Company required the site for the extension of the railway. A new site was acquired between Lea Road and The Tenters, where a new school was built for 350 children at a cost of £2,500, designed by a Mr Kirby. The foundation stone was laid by the Earl of Denbigh on 25 July 1893. Three months later, the school inspectors found it a 'good school' congratulating the managers upon the new building.[15] By 1898 there were 332 children on the books and the school

St Mary's School, Lea Road, which opened in 1893 and served until the new school was built in 1975.

Some of the pupils and staff of St Mary's School in 1895.

was found to be 'in very good order, well-maintained and efficient. The teaching was deemed sound with writing especially exceedingly good.'[16] By now, there was a new venture, 'for some time past the boys at St Mary's Catholic School, through the thoughtfulness of Mgr Slaughter have been receiving drill training — certainly a step in the right direction.'[17]

The Twentieth Century

The school went from strength to strength and by the turn of the century, its annual operatic performances were becoming a feature in Wrexham's calendar. The *Flower Queen* was performed in 1898 to a very large audience, followed in 1903 by *Caractacus* in the Public Hall in aid of St Mary's Schools. In 1906, it was *Snow White and the Seven Dwarfs*. The cast included Masters McDermott and Crewe. The 1907 production, *Dick Whittington* was reviewed in the *Wrexham Advertiser*, 23 March 1907:

> … as on previous occasions the hall proved inadequate to accommodate the large assemblage and long before the commencement, every seat was occupied, many being unable to procure admission. The audience included the Bishop of Menevia, Mr and Mrs Nelson of Acton Park, Mr and Mrs Yorke of Erddig, the Mayor and ex-mayor of Wrexham. Master Crewe played the part of Dick Whittington — (clearly a talented boy). Each displayed a confidence which was remarkable when the age of the performers was taken into consideration.

The grand sacred opera, *Ben Hur*, was performed in 1908, with John McDermott in the title role — another talented boy, while Master Crewe played the part of Rumpelstiltskin in 1910.[18]

The managers of the school in the early part of the century were Fr. Quinn, chair, George Bate, John Beirne and Michael Burke. They reported on 11 November 1903 that school numbers were growing steadily and that they were taught with dedication and zeal. The children were very happy and well looked after by their teachers. By now, Sr. Bernard was head of the juniors and Sr. Austen, head of the infant school. The 1905 HMI Report spoke of the school's excellent spirit and reported that Blanche Osborne of 38 Poyser Street had been appointed as a supplementary teacher at a salary of £30 per annum.[19]

A glimpse into the log books gives us a flavour of the school at the beginning of the twentieth century. In 1908, there was no school on Tuesday afternoon, 30 October, because of the annual tea for poor children. On account of poverty, disease was common. A child died of diphtheria and another was sent to

A group of St Mary's pupils in 1924.

hospital. The children worked hard during the term and on 17 December, the school closed for the Christmas holidays, but not before the prizes were distributed by Fr. Quinn, in the presence of Reverend Mother. Not surprisingly the children went home in great spirits.

During April 1909, the average attendance at school was 103. Empire Day was celebrated by a half-day holiday. The school was decorated and the children sang national anthems, marching round the school carrying small flags.

In June, there was a measles epidemic and the school was ordered to close.

In December, 'Mr Collins gave 4 doz nicely dressed dolls for distribution at Xmas. This generous gift should help increase attendance. By Christmas Eve the weather was severe. Fr. Quinn distributed the prizes & in spite of the weather, very few children absent.' The dressed dolls had done the trick!

The entry for 15 March 1912 mentions 'two cases scarlet fever. Coal strike gives the children a pinched look already. Rev. Manager trying to see what can be done to help them'.

On Empire Day in May, the children had instruction on the Empire. Marched round playground and sang God Save the King and in October the children presented Miss Loftus with a clock on the occasion of her marriage. Miss Loftus became Mrs Sullivan. Mrs Margaret Scott, later a teacher in the school remembers Mrs Sullivan, 'My teacher in the babies'. She began as a pupil-teacher in 1899 and taught at the school until she retired in 1949. She died in the nineteen-nineties, aged 100.

The log book continues:

Nov 21 Av[erage] att[endance] still low; several children absent for want of boots.
1914 St David's Day — children sang some Welsh songs & Rev. E. Hope spoke to them of St David.
Oct School yr ended Av att for year 130.
Oct 23 The little ones brought up 10/- for the Belgian refugees
Nov 13 We have been asked to make a collection among the children to send presents to the soldiers at the front.[20]

Between 1910 and 1920, on account of a further increase in numbers, three extra classrooms were added.

The late Frank More came to Wrexham in 1923, aged five.

I started school in the Infants Department. The building was quite long and there were two playgrounds, one of which was for the Infants Department. At right angles to the main building was another one known as 'the cookery.' In the second playground was a wooden hut which housed pupils of, say, nine and ten years old.

The pupils were a mixture of English and Welsh parentage, others possibly second generation Irish — I recall some Irish surnames. There were at least two Italian families. There were a few non-Catholic children attending the school. One of my memories is being taught Welsh by an Irish nun, Sr. Rita. There were 3 infant classes and seven in the senior school with perhaps a total of 400 children. One example of poverty between the two wars is a memory of local police officers providing boots and shoes for some children.

In the years when I was there, 1923–31, both infants & seniors heads were nuns, in addition to three other nun-teachers, Srs Pauline, Rita & Clare. The infant head was Sr. Aquinas and the lay teachers were the Misses Doherty, Miss Maloney and Miss Moran. The senior heads were successively Sr. Bernard and Sr. Trea.

At that time, the majority left school at fourteen and boys found employment as delivery boys, or were apprenticed as carpenters, electricians or plumbers, while others found employment in the 1930s at the newly-opened Marks & Spencer and Woolworths stores.

Events which stood out for Frank More were the Christmas concerts and parties and the visit of Mother General from Bordeaux.

> We were all taught to greet her with '*Bienvenu ma Mere*'. Each Friday afternoon a banner was awarded to the class with the highest attendance for the week. The prize was double playtime on one afternoon the following week. On First Fridays, senior school classes assembled for devotions to the Sacred Heart of Jesus. On holy days, children went from school to church for Mass and then dispersed. After the First Holy Communion Mass, the children went to school for breakfast.
>
> During the 1930s, as well as Srs Trea and Aquinas, there was also Sr. Clare, who was good with needlework, Sr. Rita and Sr. Pauline. Then there were Miss Downey, Miss Caffrey and Miss Smith, who took the scholarship class and was very strict.
>
> The school was successful at sports, winning the swimming shields and entered the local Eisteddfod. On Presentation Day, the Bishop gave out prayer books for Religious Instruction.[21]

On 1 September 1939, began the mass evacuation of women and children from Merseyside to north Wales. Altogether there were to be 79,000 children, and Wrexham and east Denbighshire was scheduled to receive 12,000.[22] Plans were put in place to accommodate these children, many of whom were Catholics. A double shift system was envisaged, so that local children would receive instruction for a period of four hours, from nine till one each day and the visiting children were to be instructed for four hours in the afternoon. In Wrexham, the Town Clerk liaised with Monsignor Nightingale regarding arrangements for Catholic children. So it was that St Anne's School, Liverpool came to share St Mary's School with the local Catholic children.[23]

After the war, numbers

Left: Mrs Rebecca Angus (left) and some pupils of St Mary's School in the 1950s. Mrs Angus later became headmistress of St Anne's School, Queen's Park.

Right: A group of pupils in the 1950s.

continued to increase and the 1950s were marked by serious overcrowding in the school. By 1954, there were 500 children in the school and the facilities did not meet the needs, especially of the 11+ age group. A new nursery school was added in 1956 for the youngest children, but Sr. Norbert, the headmistress, stressed the need for a two-form entry secondary school to accommodate 250 children. In spite of the overcrowding the children in the Junior Department received a thorough grounding in the basic subjects, while in the Senior Department, specialisation occurred in the teaching of geography, history, music, needlework, art and physical education. The scheme of work in history and geography involved local studies, supplying the pupils with a Welsh cultural background. In the sphere of music at this time, the school specialised in plain song, and training was aided by a tape-recorder, a recent innovation. Senior girls received instruction in cooking, cleaning, laundry, needlework and gardening, with dressmaking under Sr. Stanislaus. In sport, the school had a high record of achievement and were winners at netball, swimming and the all-age schools athletic trophy.[24]

By the end of the 1950s, space continued to be a problem and about fifty pupils attended Oteley House, the Convent of the Little Sisters of the Assumption for their lessons, while the senior girls were taught chiefly at St Mary's Institute, Bradley Road.[25] Three new classrooms were built to accommodate the school's 650 children and a neighbouring building was acquired and converted into what was described as a 'magnificent dining hall plus assembly hall.' By this time, there was a staff of twenty-two teachers, including six sisters. But still, pressure on the school was intense and plans were going ahead for the provision of a Catholic Secondary Modern School. By now there were altogether some 800 Catholic children in Wrexham.[26] But being a pupil at St Mary's was not all work. A contingent from St Mary's joined girls from the Convent School on a pilgrimage to Lourdes in April 1958.[27]

Music has always held an important place in the school. The infants put on a musical entertainment on 23 July 1958, to show the various aspects of musical activity in the school, linked with drama and on Friday, 3 July 1959, a school concert was held at the New Memorial Hall, Wrexham at a charge of 2*s*. 6*d*. This concert included class singing, including Welsh songs and there were recorders, action songs, percussion, a gypsy dancer and a play.[28]

Interviewed by the *Wrexham Leader* in early 1960 the headmistress, Sr. Norbert, said that she had known and worked in Wrexham for twenty years. She had been an assistant at the school from 1946, before becoming head in 1951. There were now six sisters in the school, 700 pupils and a teaching staff of twenty-two.[29] With the opening of St Joseph's in 1960, children of secondary school age were transferred, and St Mary's continued as a primary

St Mary's School football team, winners of the William Aston Cup, 1979–80 with Mr Brendan McDonald.

St Mary's School pupils.

Above: Mrs Margaret Coope's class in 1989.

Right: Mrs Barbara More's class, 1990 Mrs Irene Dennis on the right.

Below: Mrs Zelma Roberts (left) and Mrs Debbie Davies and the playgroup,1991.

school. Conditions in the school were still primitive by present-day standards; there was no hot running water. In 1965, an outbreak of dysentery among 167 pupils prompted yet another extension of the school. This became known as 'Top Block' at the Tenter's Square end of the complex.

Children at the school were very sad to hear in November 1969 of the death of Sr. Pauline, one of the school's best-loved teachers, at the age of 84. She had spent over sixty-one years in Wrexham altogether, forty-one of those teaching at St Mary's. She had been devoted to her work in the school and had made the parish of St Mary's the hub of her life in the firm belief that the Church had a message to bring to people.[30]

By 1972, plans began to come to fruition to build a completely new school on the site at a cost of £100,000. The children, 540 of them by now, were transferred temporarily to the recently-vacated Convent School in Grosvenor Road, while the eighty-year-old St Mary's was demolished and the new school began to be built. The children moved into the new school on 21 April 1975 and its official opening took place the following year.[31]

In July 1980, Sr. Norbert, Headmistress, retired after teaching for 35 years at the school. A musical evening was the occasion to give parents and friends the opportunity to thank her for all she had done in the school and in the parish and to see the presents to which they had contributed. She also received a cheque and a trip to Rome from the parish. She was replaced by Mr Mike Greaney, who would remain as Head until 1999. By now, there were 387 children on the roll, all looking very smart in their uniforms.[32]

Features of the school year during the 1980s, as well as normal classes, was the regular Mass in the school celebrated by Fr. Morgan, the First Communions, the introduction of a Youth Club and the formation of a Parent-Teachers Association in 1981. There were visits to the Police Station, Liverpool Cathedral, Chester Zoo, the ballet at Theatr Clwyd and, further afield, a trip by private train to York. The Head's comment was heartfelt 'a wonderful day, without any problems'. There was fundraising for Help the Aged and for a therapy pool at Powys Special School. The school choir sang regularly at the Cathedral and pupils gained two distinctions at Chester Music Festival.

One highlight was the visit of Bishop Ward, an old boy of the school, after he was ordained co-adjutor to Bishop Fox. The Mass at the Cathedral the following day for the children at St Mary's and St Joseph's, was 'a wonderful occasion'.

But there were problems to contend with. The threatened spending cuts in education were not averted. Despite a mass demo-nstration at Shirehall, the school had to lose two teachers and the classes had to be reshuffled. By the end of the 1980s, a

St Mary's pupils dressed in Victorian costume to celebrate the centenary of the school on the Lea Road site in 1993.

St Mary's School staff, early 1990s. The headteacher, Mr Mike Greaney, seated fourth from right.

group of travellers' children had joined the school and had integrated well.[33]

The highlight of the 1990s were the celebrations surrounding the centenary of St Mary's on the Lea Road site in 1993.

> A tremendous amount of planning and work has gone into preparing the Centenary Celebrations. The whole school now houses an exhibition depicting the history of both St Mary's and the local area and all classes have contributed. At 7pm on Mon, Tues, Wed & Thrs our concert, "The way we were", will be staged, written by Mrs Moira Catherall, Deputy Head.

The last performance was staged before an invited audience including Archbishop Ward, Bishop Hannigan, the Director of Education, the Mayor and Mayoress of Wrexham and many priests and nuns associated with the school over the years.

Despite the fact that the school was by now serving seven parishes, there had been a gradual reduction in numbers of pupils, from 390 in 1992 to 353 in 1995. The visit of Her Majesty's Inspectors in 1995 found the overall standards of achievement in the majority of subjects satisfactory to good, with provision for under-fives good. They found the school a happy one with good relations between pupils, parents and staff. Good manners, politeness and mutual respect were clearly evident, they said.[34]

In 1997, Mike Greaney left to become Diocesan Schools Commissioner and Mrs Kathy Jones replaced him as Head.

The school hit the headlines of the *Wrexham Leader* in 1999, when what was described as 'an exciting video and internet project' was launched called, 'A Childs' Vision' creating a picture of the future as seen by infant and junior school children, who were encouraged to explore how scientific advances will affect towns and the natural world. Dr Cornford from NEWI said, 'It is hoped that the childrens' message will be a powerful reminder to all of us of our own responsibility to ensure that the world in which we live will be fit for these and future children.[35]

St Mary's School pupils.

Above: Mrs Margaret Coope's class,1992.

Left: Mrs Margaret Coope's class, 1995.

Below: In fancy dress, 1990s.

St Mary's School pupils at Wrexham General Station, 1950s, departing for Lourdes.

St Mary's continued to do well into the new Millenium. They won a trio of awards in 2001 — an Eco-Award for commitment to the environment, an Investors in People Award for commitment to staff and pupil development and a Basic Skills Award for its educational standards. The same year brought glowing praise from her Majesty's Inspectors. St Mary's was described as a 'well-managed properly organised school, which exudes a warm, welcoming positive ethos'.[36]

In the following year, the children raised more than £100 for a special project supporting schools in Africa. Among other activities in 2004, was the collection of 190 shoe boxes of gifts for Operation Xmas Child. The following year, the pupils pledged their support for recycling by adding their thumbprints to a poster produced by Waste Awareness Wales. The children must have been delighted in 2006, when a new school playground was laid for them.

The school continues to grow and to develop. The occasion of the extension of the European Union has meant that children from Poland, Portugal and other countries have become pupils at St Mary's. It is hoped that the school will continue its long tradition of 'good manners, politeness and mutual respect'[36] for all so clearly evident today and that they will continue to grow into responsible citizens making a positive contribution to the town of Wrexham and to the wider world.

St Joseph's High School

One issue which loomed large during the first half of Bishop Petit's time was that of providing secondary education for Catholic children. The Butler Education Act of 1944, providing free secondary education for all meant a vast reorganisation of educational provision throughout the country. Local Education Authorities were required to submit development plans, showing their intended reconstruction.

Against a backdrop of growing numbers of Catholics in north Wales as elsewhere, the local authorities, consisting mainly of Nonconformists tended to regard Catholic schools as places of propaganda and indoctrination. 'The hostility to Catholic requests to be included in these plans was fervent.'[38] 'Hostility towards Catholic proposals occurred more frequently in Menevia than in any other British diocese.'[39]

When the Menevia Diocesan Education Committee objected in 1954 to being omitted from the development plan for Wrexham, the Denbighshire Education Authority resolved that the Ministry of Education be informed that, in view of the facilities which the authority intended to provide for secondary education in the Wrexham district, the committee considered it educationally unsound to provide a one-stream Catholic secondary modern school in Wrexham. Despite the Ministry of Education's advising careful consideration be given to the proposal of the Catholic authorities, the Reorganisation Committee felt that they were unable to recommend such a course of action. 'It was pointed out that the school was not needed either because of overcrowding to the degree of uncomfortableness in present schools or because of a reorganisation of rural schools.'[40] The same edition of the paper reported that a deputation from Denbighshire Education Committee was to meet with the Minister of Education to discuss a proposal to provide a £100,000 Roman Catholic Secondary Modern School at Wrexham.

Eighteen months later, the Denbighshire Education Committee removed their objections to a Catholic school in Wrexham and it was proposed to provide one to cater for 300 children at a cost of £93,000. Eventually the school was built and Thursday, 24 November 1960 saw its official opening by Bishop Beck of Salford, Chairman of the Catholic Education Council. An address was given by the Director of Education, T. Glyn Davies and during the ceremony, a choir sang a carol written by Richard

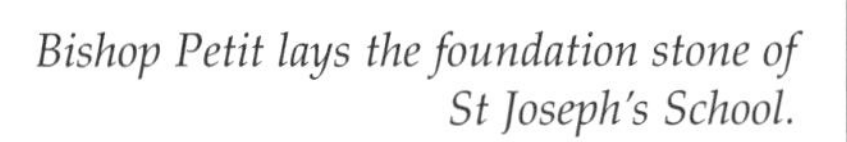

Bishop Petit lays the foundation stone of St Joseph's School.

Below: The school nears completion.

The original staff of St Joseph's School with Bishop Petit, Mr J. M. Cleary (headteacher) and Father Breen.

Gwyn, while in gaol in Wrexham, before his martyrdom in 1584. In his address, Bishop Beck said it was illogical and short-sighted to heavily penalise the Catholic community for trying to get closer links between home and school. 'We believe that education can only attain its high ideals if there is a close harmony between home and school.[41] He concluded by referring to the 'enormous self-sacrifice' of the Catholic community, particularly where new schools had to be built. 'It was an enormous programme', he said.

Until this time, St Mary's all-age school had served Wrexham's Catholic community. With the opening of St Joseph's, the senior pupils of St Mary's were transferred there. Ultimately, the new school cost £113,000, of which the Catholic authorities had to provide £57,000. The Denbighshire Education Authority provided a grant of £12,000 and the Ministry of Education, £44,000. The Catholics of Wrexham had to find a huge sum of money and hence all the fund-raising schemes in the following years. Mr J. M. Cleary, who had previously taught in Cardiff was appointed headteacher of the new school and three Holy Family Sisters joined the staff.

By 1964 , it was decided to convert St Joseph's into a bi-lateral school, thus providing a grammar school education for a small number of pupils.[42] The end of the sixties saw 230 on the school roll and there were plans to make it a comprehensive school, taking in some of the Catholic pupils who were currently at state grammar schools in the area. It was also to cater for those girls at the Convent Grammar School at its closure in 1972.

By the early 1970s St Joseph's fitted into the Wrexham Education complex, with its new head, Mr John Thompson. As one of the seven 11–16 comprehensive schools, small compared to others in the area, it would send its pupils to either Yale or the Denbighshire Technical College for further studies. By 1976, St Joseph's was offering its 450 pupils a choice of twelve subjects at GCE 'O' Level and CSE.

The school aimed to provide a Christian education, in partnership with parents and parishes in an atmosphere of understanding, tolerance and support in which each pupil would have a full Catholic experience, an educational experience of quality relevant to his/her needs and abilities and all pupils would be encouraged to witness to Christ in their lives.[43] It seems that the school was fulfilling these aims, for during the 1990s, Clwyd County Council spoke of the school's 'high level of success' with a good standard of achievement in classes and in the numbers of pupils achieving A*–C grades in public exams. They are significantly higher than local and national averages.' The report also spoke of 'a good relationship between pupils and teachers.'

Furthermore, they rated St Joseph's as having 'a high level of success in regard to the pupils' 'spiritual, moral, social and cultural development', commending the caring attitude of the staff and 'the strong Christian philosophy and principles'.[44] The children were working hard. By 1997, the schools Homework Club had the biggest intake for any school in Wrexham and was a 'big hit with pupils and teachers'.[45] By now, St Joseph's had 470 on the school roll, drawing pupils from a wide catchment area. In January 1997, Mr John Kenworthy took over as headteacher on Mr John Thompson's retirement.

By 2003, the school was celebrating the 'Best in Wales' award for making the most improvement in its examination successes.[46]

But life at St Joseph's has never been all work. The school won local netball tournaments back in 1963 and 1964.[47] In 1966, the first year that St Joseph's had entered the scheme, some of the boys were bronze medal winners in the Duke of Edinburgh's Award Scheme. In the same year, golf was introduce into the school curriculum.[48] Three years later, the boys' athletic team were winners of the Tucker Cup at the County Sports held at Colwyn Bay. They were congratulated for being an outstanding Secondary Modern School.[49]

More recently, Laura Watson, who has Down's Syndrome, won four medals, including a gold at the West Midlands Regional Athletics championships held in Birmingham in 2004, when she was sixteen. For many years a supporter of Wrexham FC, she was the official mascot for Wrexham's home game against Luton when she was thirteen.

Music, too, has been an important part of the school's life. By 1966 guitar lessons were given by Sr. Eucharia, while Mr Ellis, a violin tutor, visited the school every Friday.[50]

In 1967, under the headline 'Leavers prepare for the adult world', the *Leader* ran an article about a six-week project to give pupils a taste of what life after school might be like. It was a very practical scheme. The pupils organised themselves into groups, which among other activities, some made rugs for old people's homes, while others knitted babywear. A biology

A group of pupils with a sister in the corridor at St Joseph's.

pool was built, the school playing field was fenced off and a rabbit hutch was made for the Biology Department. The girls visited factories on the Wrexham Trading Estate, while the boys went to Brymbo Steelworks, the GPO Sorting Office and Gresford Colliery.

In 1968, the Head introduced the idea of community service for the older pupils and by 1970, Thursday afternoons were set aside by the fourteen to fifteen year olds in Form 4b for this. It mainly entailed helping old people in various ways. One of the boys, Peter Lane said 'The lady I visit used to be a schoolteacher. She is now in her 80s and she usually has a job or two for me to do.' The *Leader* dubbed the pupils 'Good Samaritans All' under the headline, 'Meet the kids who care and show it.'[51]

Ten years ago (1997), St Joseph's School formed a Young Enterprise Group called Regalia and won a clutch of awards. Among other projects, the girls made jewellery and Regalia was voted the best company by Wrexham Young Enterprise Board. They won a cup for the Best Company Public Relations and the Best Company Presentation.[52]

But the school looked even further afield. From the mid-eighties, there have been student exchanges with a school in Germany. In 2002, three teachers and thirty-seven pupils from Bergstadt Gymnasium in Ludenscheid, Germany came to spend a week at St Joseph's, which according to everyone, was highly successful.[53] Over the years, there has been much growth and development in the school, but perhaps the most exciting development began to get underway as the new century opened. St Joseph's has now been developed into a joint Anglican and Roman Catholic secondary school.

The vision for the shared school includes a commitment to proclaim a clear Christian message, based on Gospel values to offer, to both children and parents in Wrexham and district, an unique Christian education — a learning community based upon the values of the Christian faith, to be fully Catholic and fully Church-in-Wales and serve as a witness to Our Lord Jesus Christ, celebrating the strengths and respecting the differences of both traditions. At a cost of £8,500,000 the former St Joseph's School has been extended to cope

The children take part in the ceremony to open the new St Joseph's School in 2006.

with the estimated intake of about 600 pupils, with 85% of the funding coming from the National Assembly and 15% from the Church-in-Wales.

St Joseph's Catholic and Anglican High School was opened during an intensely busy week at the end of November 2006. On Monday, 27 November, the spiritual opening of the school took place. Bishop Regan, Roman Catholic Bishop of Wrexham and Bishop John Davies, Anglican Bishop of St Asaph officiated jointly at a service which included the blessing of the new chapel. On the following Thursday, 30 November 2006, Wales' first shared-faith school welcomed Jane Davidson, Minister of Education and Lifelong Learning to open the school.[54]

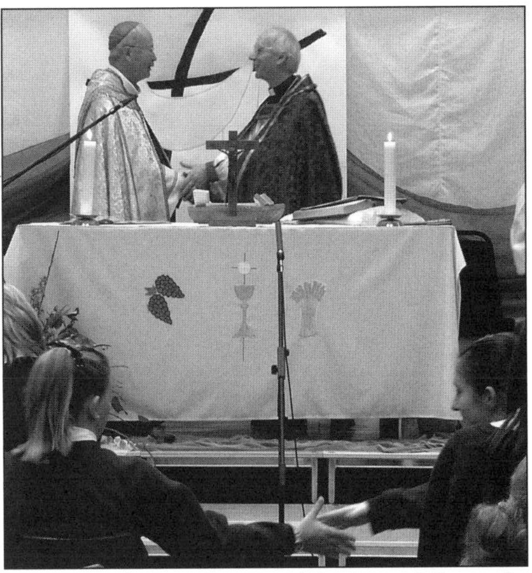

Bishops Regan and Davies, and the pupils, link hands at the spiritual opening of the new St Joseph's School.

The school now looks to the future. 'Almost 600 pupils, Catholic, Anglican and other faiths will experience an education in which Christianity, prayer and worship are key features.'[55] In the words of the final prayer said at the opening of the school chapel:

> Whenever we gather in this school and beyond it, in our homes, we ask you to enlighten the eyes of our hearts and minds. Help us to be a real community, loving and supporting each other, on our journey of faith together. Amen.[56]

Convent Grammar School

Soon after the Holy Family Sisters took up their duties at St Mary's Catholic schools in 1879, they opened a High School at their convent at 22 Regent Street. By 1889, the Sisters received 'a limited number of young ladies for private lessons in music, painting, drawing, singing and modern languages.[57] By 1891, there were seven sisters altogether, three of them teaching in the Convent High School. The Headmistress was Sr. St John, from Ireland. She was helped by Sr. Ursula, also from Ireland and Sr. Anastasia from London.[58] The school must have been a success for they were looking for larger premises and helped by the bishop, they purchased Bron Llwyn, a 'substantial private residence' in Grosvenor Road.[59]

The following advertisement appeared in the *Wrexham Advertiser* on 1 January 1898:

> Convent High School for young ladies Under the patronage of His Lordship, the Rt Rev. Dr Mostyn, Vicar Apostolic of Wales. The Sisters beg to announce that they have removed to Grosvenor Road and are now prepared to receive a larger number of young ladies. For prospectuses apply to the Superioress.[60]

By 1914, the number of children at the school must again have increased, for they built an annexe in the grounds, which became known as the Bungalow. The next forty years was a story of expansion. By 1923, they purchased the adjacent property, 17 Grosvenor Road, and in 1937 they bought 2 Gerald Street. By the 1940s, there were twelve sisters working in

Two of the Victorian houses which formed the basis of the Convent School on Grosvenor Road.

the Convent High School. Sister Angelica was the headmistress, while Rev. Mother Clothilde was the Superioress of the community.[61] Marjorie Dakin, a pupil at the school from 1938–48 remembers Sr. Angelica as being 'strict, dignified, but fair.' Other staff included Sr. Gertrude, Sr. Salome and Sr. Enda. The war years impacted on the pupils' education. There were no science lessons because of a shortage of teachers and no domestic science because of food rationing. Marjorie remembers the iron railings being cut down for the war effort and going to the pro-Cathedral to give thanks for the end of the war. The children at the school were 'polite and well-mannered and adhered to quite a strict régime'. Another pupil attending the school just after the war remembers everywhere 'being highly polished. Pupils had to keep everywhere tidy and clean.' By this time, the Headmistress was Sr. Cyril. An outstanding event during her time at the school was the visit of the Mother General from Canada.

Margaret James, who later joined the WRNS, remembers Sr. Cyril as being 'very strict and stood no nonsense, but got results; she also taught general science.' Other staff included Sr. Salome (French and music), Mrs Cook (English), Mrs McGoran (mathematics), Sr. Enda (Latin), Sr. Peter (cookery and needlework) and Mrs Griffiths (sports). A memorable event during her time was the inspection for the school to be recognised as a grammar school. Altogether she found it a very happy school, ' more of a family than a school.' Her memories of her time at the school included the foreign trips to Rome, Switzerland and Lourdes, taking part in the Richard Gwyn processions, walking from the Beast Market to the Cathedral, sports days and netball tournaments. 'Every Corpus Christi we went to Carrog and made the Stations of the Cross on the hillside. I thoroughly enjoyed my time at the school and feel that I was very lucky to have had the opportunity to go there.' Ann Clough remembers the frequent visits of a very jovial Canon Evans — a marvellous artist. She has enduring memories of 'hot summers, when we had windows open and we wore green summer dresses, blazers and straw hats.' A fine tribute to the school is the fact that

Above: Domestic Science class, 1950s.

Left: Convent School staff, 1972. Back row L–R: –?–; Mrs McGoran; Mrs Shirin Nelson; Mrs Humphries; –?–. Front row: Sister Salome; Sister Enda (headmistress); –?–.

Below: A group of pupils, dressed in full uniform, complete with hats, in 1964–5

A group of pupils photographed with Mrs Humphries in 1968.

over fifty years later a group of 'girls' meet regularly for lunch and are still good friends and it was they who kindly shared the above information with me.

In 1949, a canteen and a domestic science building were erected. In 1951, the nursery and junior school were accommodated at 6 Gerald Street. This allowed for major alterations to the main building. In 1952 'considerable structural alterations were carried out, four large classrooms, a fully equipped laboratory and a pleasant school library were provided.'[62] The object was to apply to the Ministry of Education for recognition as a grammar school and a preparatory school and by August 1954, they had achieved that ambition. By now it admitted boys in the Preparatory Department and Sr. Enda was Headmistress (1953–72).

Throughout its life, the school had the financial support of the Holy Family Order, but by the 1960s , the Convent School was finding things more and more difficult. New buildings were needed and there was neither the land nor the money to build them. On the opening of St Joseph's School in 1960, three Sisters were appointed to the staff.

Sr. Elizabeth, now housekeeper at Bishop's House, taught science at the school between 1963 and 1965. By then, there were three sisters on the staff and about eight lay staff. She

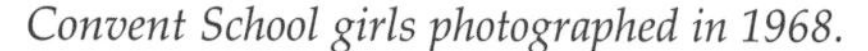

Convent School girls photographed in 1968.

remembers that 'there were about 190 Catholics. The Catholic pupils who passed the 11+ were admitted to the school at no cost (the LEA would not give us anything so we educated the girls as part of our community sharing). The school had a good name and we had good relations with St Mary's.[64]

Holy Family sisters, photographed at the Convent School c.1969.

Lack of both personnel and financial resources threatened closure by 1970, but this was held back as the reorganisation of education in the area meant that St Joseph's school, built in 1960 as a secondary modern school could develop into a comprehensive school. This would be able to offer former pupils from the Convent School an equivalent education. So, in 1972, the school closed its doors for the last time. For over eighty years, boys as well as girls had been given a good education within its walls. 'It was the end of an era, but the school had served its purpose, and that is what matters.'[65]

References

1. Catholic Directory.
2. *Wrexham Advertiser,* 1 October 1851.
3. DODD, Charles, *Wrexham Schools and Scholars*, 1924.
4. Ibid.
5. Ibid.
6. Ibid.
7. *Wrexham Advertiser,* 26 August 1869.
8. Ibid.
9. DODD, op cit.
10. Garden fete programme, 1931.
11. DODD, op cit.
12. *Wrexham Advertiser,* 17 June 1871.
13. SHREWSBURY DIOCESAN ARCHIVES, Educational statistics of the diocese of Shrewsbury, 1874 .
14. DODD, op cit.
15. Ibid.
16. *Wrexham Advertiser,* 5 November 1898.
17. Ibid, 17 September 1898.
18. *Wrexham Advertiser, passim.*
19. DRO/ED/MB/101/7, St Mary's RC School Managers' Minutes, 1903–06.
20. DRO/ED/MB/101/7, St Mary's Log Books, 1908–52.
21. Frank More's Memoirs.
22. *Wrexham Leader,* 1 September 1939.
23. Borough of Wrexham Minutes, 1939–40.
24. *Wrexham Advertiser and Star*, 25 May 1954.
25. *Wrexham Leader,* 15 January 1960.
26. *Menevia Record,* November 1957

27. *Wrexham Leader,* 8 April 1958.
28. Ibid, July 1959.
29. Ibid, 15 January 1960.
30. *Wrexham Gazette,* 27 November 1969.
31. *Wrexham Leader,* 1972 .
32. Log Books.
33. Ibid.
34. Ibid.
35. *Wrexham Leader,* 1999 .
36. HM Inspection, 2001.
37. Ibid, 1995.
38. *Western Mail,* 8 March 1960.
39. HUGHES, Trystan, *Winds of Change,* 1999, p151.
40. *Wrexham Leader,* 30 December 1955.
41. *Western Mail,* 25 November 1960.
42. *Liverpool Daily Post,* 7 April 1964.
43. Mission Statement 1994-5.
44. A. N. Palmer Centre, Wrexham press-cuttings file.
45. *Evening Leader,* 19 January 1997.
46. *Wrexham Leader,* 7 March 2003.
47. Ibid, 16 October 1964.
48. *Wrexham Leader,* 26 April 1969.
49. *Wrexham Gazette,* 26 June 1966.
50. Ibid, 14 July 1967.
51. *Wrexham Leader,* 24 March 1970.
52. *Wrexham Leader,* 13 June 1997.
53. *Evening Leader,* 16 May 2002.
54. Official Opening Programme, 30 November 2006
55. www. wrexham. gov. uk/english/council/news/stjosephs. stm.
56. The Blessing of our new Chapel, 27 November 2006.
57. *Wrexham Advertiser,* 10 August 1889.
58. Census 1891.
59. WILLIAMS, W. Alister, *Encyclopaedia of Wrexham,* 2001.
60. *Wrexham Advertiser,* 1 January 1898.
61. Bishop Hannan's Visitation, 1942.
62. *Menevia Record,* 1952.
63. *The Holy Family Sisters in Wrexham, 1879–1979,* 1979.
64. Sister Elizabeth's Recollections.
65. *The Holy Family Sisters in Wrexham, 1879–1979,* 1979.

CHAPTER NINE

The Clergy

Bishops

At the time of the Reformation, Wrexham was part of the diocese of St Asaph. Bishop Thomas Goldwell was its bishop from 1555–9. Under Queen Elizabeth, the Catholic Church was outlawed and its hierarchy became extinct. Unable to accept the new church régime, Bishop Goldwell fled to the Continent in the summer of 1559, never to return to Wales.

It was to be 130 years till anything resembling normal church government for Catholics was introduced. On 30 January 1688, Pope Innocent XI appointed four bishops, each responsible for one of four areas of England and Wales — the London District, the Midland District, the Northern District and the Western District. These bishops each had the title of Vicar-Apostolic. Wrexham lay in the Western District which, as well as covering the whole of Wales included what are now the dioceses of Plymouth and Clifton.

The first Vicar-Apostolic of the Western District was a Benedictine monk, **Dom Michael Ellis, OSB, (1688–1708)**, who was consecrated on 6 May 1688 in St James' Palace. Known as a popular preacher, he was the convert son of a Protestant clergyman. Hopes were running high among Catholics, hoping for a change in their fortunes, as they had suffered much for their faith. According to a newsletter dated 31 July 1688, at the same time that the Vicars Apostolic of the Northern and Midland Districts visited those districts, Bishop Ellis was 'going towards Wales' to preside in his district and 'inspect those of the Romish persuasion.'[1] So Bishop Ellis made at least one brief visit to Wales. Hopes were dashed by the autumn, by which time King James II had been deposed and exiled. Bishop Ellis and later Bishop Giffard of the Midland District were imprisoned in Newgate. On his release, Bishop Ellis made his way to Rome and although he wished to do so, he was destined never to return to his see. In 1705, he resigned, becoming Bishop of Segni, a diocese he served for eighteen years. Morale among Catholics, especially in Wales, was very low and with no bishop, very few priests and little sacramental life, numbers dwindled.[2]

It was not until 1713 that another Vicar Apostolic was appointed for the Western District. This time it was a Franciscan, **Bishop Matthew Prichard OFM, (1715–50)**, who was appointed. Born at Graig near Abergavenny in 1669, of a prosperous recusant family, he was ordained in 1693 and was a scholar, teaching philosophy and theology at Louvain University for twelve years. The whole of his life as a bishop was spent in the vicinity of his birthplace. We might know more about him had the archives of the Western District not been destroyed during the Gordon Riots in Bath in 1780. He had the reputation of being a quiet man, but proved himself a man of action when he undertook a journey to Rome in 1736, seeking financial help for his poor district. He died at the age of 81 and was succeeded by Bishop York, who had been his co-adjutor.[3]

Bishop Wiliam Lawrence York, OSB, (1750–63), had been born in London in 1687, but had connections with Bath where was to spend time both as a missioner and as a bishop. Again, he was an order priest, this time a Benedictine, having been professed at St Gregory's Douai. Ordained in 1711, he was Prior of St Edmund's, Paris, 1721–5 and prior of his own monastery, 1725–9. From 1730, he was in charge of the mission at Bath, living in Bell-Tree House. He was consecrated as co-adjutor to Bishop Prichard at St Gregory's, Douai in 1741. He succeeded Bishop Prichard as Vicar-Apostolic of the Western District on 22 May 1750. Like Bishop Prichard, he seems to have had a quiet, retiring nature, befitting the times which were still potentially dangerous for Catholics. Little is known about his ministry for lack of surviving records, but it is known that he administered confirmation, which is to be expected , in various corners of his huge district. In a letter to Rome in 1747, he told of the distressing state of affairs, which he as a bishop found himself in at that time. 'We are compelled to fly from house to house, from city to city. Bishop Prichard is ill, I his unworthy co-adjutor have been a fugitive from my ordinary residence and as yet I have no fixed abode.'[4] Persecution was incessant and the extent of the vicariate was enormous — 60 miles long and 180 miles wide. In 1764, he retired to his monastery in Douai and died in 1770, while he was celebrating Mass.[5]

Bishop Charles Walmsley OSB, (1763–97), Bishop of Rama, his co-adjutor succeeded him. A Lancashire Catholic, he was born in 1722, one of twelve children of John Walmsley of Westwood House, Wigan. He was a pupil at St Gregory's College, Douai, going on to become a monk at St Edmund's, Paris. He was to become one of the most celebrated of the Western Vicars Apostolic. He was a Doctor of the Sorbonne and enjoyed an international reputation as a scientist. In 1750, he was elected a Fellow of the Royal Society and, having a high reputation for mathematics and astronomy, he was consulted by the British Government on the adoption of the new style Gregorian Calendar. In 1771, he published a commentary on the Apocalypse, later seeing many of his apocalyptic fears materialise. He saw his chapel and his house together with all his papers lost in a fire in the 1780 Gordon Riots. He is best remembered for consecrating John Carroll as Bishop of Baltimore in the chapel at Lulworth and is seen as the 'Godfather' of the American Hierarchy. He was known to be a deeply spiritual man. Feeble and partially blind, he died on 25 November 1797 as a result of his bath chair overturning.[6] He came to Holywell to administer confirmation to sixteen people on 2 July 1786.[7]

He was succeeded by **Bishop Gregory Sharrock, OSB,** another monk of St Gregory's, Douai, which in 1814 was to become Downside Abbey. He had been born on 30 March 1742 in Walton le Dale, near Preston, Lancashire. He was professed in 1758 and ordained in 1766. He was in turn cellarer, bursar and prior of his monastery. He was consecrated at Wardour, and came to be known as a very pastoral bishop, devoted to his scattered flock. One of his concerns was the welfare of the exiled French priests, who had become refugees on account of the French Revolution.[8]

Like any bishop, he travelled round administering the sacrament of confirmation. He came into Wales and on the 14 July 1799, he had travelled as far as Holywell where, in his diary, he noted that there was a congregation of 200 people, thirty of them from the Mostyn household at Talacre, when he confirmed sixteen 'at the star'.[9]

Bishop Peter Bernardine Collingridge, OFM, (1809-1829), Bishop of Thespiae, became his co-adjutor in 1807, and succeed him in 1809. He was a Franciscan, a friar of St Bonaventure's, Douai and had been born in Fritwell, Oxfordshire on 10 March 1757. He was a quiet, humble man, a true son of St Francis. 'Bishop Collingridge's episcopate was a fruitful one for the whole of Wales. He is referred to as a learned and saintly bishop and he saw the greatest needs of his district.'[10] He tried to establish a mission on Anglesey, but failed for want of means. He was more successful in Bangor, where a mission was established in 1827 and in Wrexham, where Catholics were provided with a chapel by 1828. For some time he lived in Cannington, Somerset. He confirmed nine at the Star, Holywell on 26 August, 1810 and another six on 21 November 1813.[11] Any Catholics in Wrexham desiring the sacrament of Confirmation would have had to make the journey to Holywell. Bishop Collingridge was to become more intimately connected with Wrexham, than his predecessors, when John Briggs, a priest based in the Chester mission, visited the area in the 1820s to see if he could find any Catholics. The few which he found were to form the tiny nucleus of the congregation for whom, in the fullness of time, a chapel would be built and a missioner appointed to nurture the little flock. He died in 1829, the same year that the Catholic Emancipation Act was passed.[12]

Bishop Peter Augustine Baines OSB, (1829–40), a controversial and flamboyant character, succeeded him. He had been born near Liverpool and was educated at Lambspring in Germany, which was the home of the English Benedictines in that country. He transferred to Ampleforth and in 1810, he was ordained. By 1817, he was in charge of the Bath mission. He was well-known as a preacher and he succeeded Bishop Collingridge in 1829, having been his co-adjutor for six years. He saw seminary training as a high priority, hoping that Downside would become a seminary for his District, but his hopes were not realised.[13]

In 1840, the ecclesiastical boundaries were re-drawn and Wales became a Vicariate in its own right remaining so until the Restoration of the Hierarchy in 1850. During this time, **Bishop Thomas Joseph Brown, OSB, (1840–80),** was Vicar-Apostolic of the Welsh District, as titular bishop of Apollonia. He had been born in Bath on 2 May 1798 and educated by the Benedictines at Acton Burnell. He was professed at Downside, near Bath, where the Douai community had moved in 1814, and he was ordained priest by Bishop Poynter on 7 April 1823. He was consecrated bishop in St John's, Bath on 28 October 1840 and lived first at Chepstow and then at Bullingham, near Hereford from where he oversaw the Welsh District, which, as well as Wales, included Herefordshire and Monmouthshire. In his first pastoral letter, he wrote:

> The field allotted to us is extensive and extremely necessitous … We have hardly a school in any of our missions wherein the faith and morals of multitudes of poor Catholic children who abound there may be formed and preserved. We have no means at our disposal. We have no seminary. We are almost without resources for the education of clergy. We, ourselves, are entirely dependent on the liberality and charity of those who can assist us.[14]

Bishop Hedley said of him 'For forty years he travelled, preached, wrote saved and begged for his flock.' In 1850 he became the bishop of Newport and Menevia.[15]

At the Restoration of the Hierarchy in 1850, the six counties of north Wales became part of the new diocese of Shrewsbury, whose bishop was **James Brown (1851–81).** He had been born in Wolverhampton on 11 January 1812 and was educated at Sedgley Park School and Oscott, where he was ordained priest on 18 February 1837. He remained at Oscott as a professor and Prefect of Studies until 1844, when he returned to Sedgley Park, where he was to become President. Under his presidency, the school flourished. He was consecrated first bishop of the new and extensive diocese of Shrewsbury on 25 July 1851. Wrexham with the six northern counties of Wales became part of his diocese, which also included Cheshire and Shropshire.[16]

When he died on 14 October 1881, he was succeeded by **Bishop Edmund Knight (1881–95)**. Educated in Walsall and at Oscott, he eventually went to the Collegio Pio in Rome, where he was ordained priest on 19 December 1857. After serving as secretary to both the Bishop of Clifton and Cardinal Wiseman, he became vice-president of Oscott and professor of moral theology. He was consecrated auxiliary Bishop of Shrewsbury on 25 July 1879 under the title of Bishop of Coricum. He was appointed to the see of Shrewsbury on 25 April 1881. Described as imbued with the spirit of St Francis de Sales, he saw education as a very high priority. He resigned his see on 11 May 1895, due to ill health and died on 9 June 1905.[17]

In 1895, the six northern counties of Wales were severed from the diocese of Shrewsbury and the rest of the Principality, except Glamorgan was removed from the Diocese of Newport and Menevia and together became the Welsh Vicariate and on 14 September 1895, **Rev. Francis Mostyn (1895–1926)** was consecrated titular bishop of Ascalon and Vicar Apostolic of Wales. In 1898, this area became the diocese of Menevia, with Bishop Mostyn as its first bishop. Menevia is a latinised form of Mynyw, the diocese of St David, patron saint of Wales. At first living in St Mary's presbytery, and then in Richmond House, Grosvenor Road, he was the first of the nine Roman Catholic bishops to reside in the town of Wrexham.

Wrexham was chosen as the bishop's seat, both on account of its being the largest town in north Wales and because of easy communication by road and by train. Francis Mostyn, born in 1860, was the son of Sir Pyers and Lady Mostyn of Talacre, Flintshire, north Wales. The Mostyns were an old Catholic family, the Bishop numbering three of the English martyrs among his ancestors. Bishop Mostyn was educated at St Mary's College, Oscott 1871–9 and St Cuthbert's College, Ushaw, 1879–84. He was ordained a priest for the diocese of Shrewsbury {of which at the time north Wales was a part} on 14 September 1884. On the 50th anniversary of the building of St Mary's in 1907, it became the pro-Cathedral of his diocese. Bishop Mostyn remained in Wrexham until 1921, when on 7 March, he was appointed second Archbishop of Cardiff, in succession to Archbishop Bilsborrow. It was said that no man travelled Wales more than he. During his episcopate in Menevia he was able to lay firm foundations on which subsequent bishops could build. There was a steady increase both in the number of Catholics and in the number of churches built. On his departure from Wrexham, the see was left vacant, Archbishop Mostyn becoming Apostolic Administrator for the whole of Wales, until the appointment of his successor in the northern diocese five years later. He died on 25 October 1939.[18]

On 8 September 1926, **Canon Francis John Vaughan (1926–35)** was consecrated as the new Bishop of Menevia by Archbishop Mostyn. A nephew of Cardinal Vaughan and a member of another old Catholic family, Bishop Vaughan was born at Courtfield, Ross-on-Wye on 5 May 1877. He was educated at the Oratory School, Caversham, St Sulpice, Paris and Ushaw. He was ordained for the old diocese of Newport on 5 July 1903 and was a curate at St Joseph's, Aberavon, 1903–09. He was in poor health for some years and then became parish priest of Barry Dock in 1914. In 1922, he was created canon of the Cardiff Chapter. On 8 September 1926, he was consecrated Bishop of Menevia in St David's Cathedral, Cardiff. In the same year, Plas Tirion, Sontley Road, Wrexham was purchased for his residence and as Bishop's House/*Ty'r Escob* has been the home of his successors ever since.

Under his leadership, there were many developments in the diocese. As a man of prayer he was delighted to welcome contemplative orders of nuns into the diocese. A gifted speaker, he was in demand outside the diocese, but used to say, 'My heart and my work are always with Wales.' During his episcopate the diocesan clergy increased from twenty-four to fifty-six and the numbers of places where Mass was celebrated increased from sixty-two to seventy-seven. The numbers of Catholics were increasing in north Wales, partly due to an influx of people from the north of England to live in Flintshire and Denbighshire and partly because, during his time about one thousand people were received into the Church in the diocese. He died suddenly on 13 March 1935 after accidentally swallowing a bone.[19]

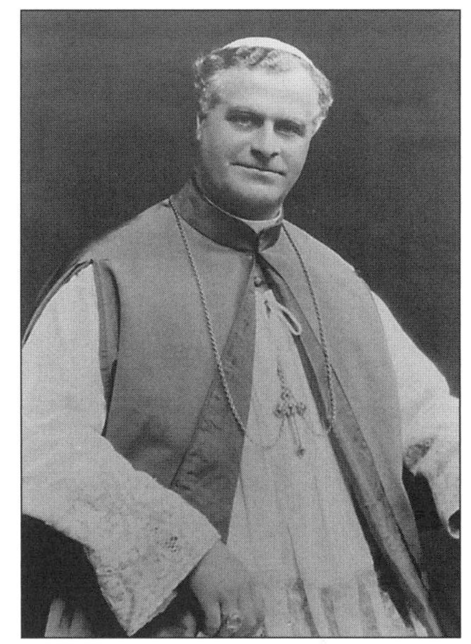

Bishop Vaughan.

Bishop Vaughan was succeeded by an Irishman, **Bishop Michael Joseph McGrath, DD, MA, LLD, (1935–40),** who was consecratedon 24 September 1935. Born on 24 March 1882 in Kilkenny, he was educated at St John's College, Waterford, the National University of Ireland and St Sulpice, Paris. He held a degree in Celtic studies and was a gifted linguist, speaking French, German, Gaelic, Welsh, Russian and Italian fluently. On coming to the Diocese of Menevia, he studied Welsh under the Aberystwyth bard, Professor Wynn Jones and described himself as a 'converted Welshman.' He was ordained for the diocese of Clifton on 12 July 1908. He was curate at Clifton pro-Cathedral until 1911, when he became Rector of St Joseph's, Fishponds, Bristol, moving to St Nicholas's Pennywell, Bristol until 1915, when he became chaplain to a girls' reformatory. In 1919, he left Clifton diocese and joined the diocese of Menevia. He was parish priest of St Mary's, Flint until 1927, when he moved to Our Lady and St Winefride's at Aberystwyth. After eighteen months, he became rector of St Mary's College, Aberystwyth, where men were trained for ministry in Wales. The college closed in 1934 and Dr McGrath went to Bangor. In less than a year he was to become Bishop of Menevia diocese and on 20 June, 1940, he was translated to Cardiff as its Archbishop. His achievements as bishop and archbishop were both 'numerous and impressive.' He opened many churches and schools and did his utmost to prevent leakage from the church, both by denouncing the evils of the day as he saw them and by providing Catholic education for Catholic children. He defended the church against denominational and secular attacks, while he gained non-Catholic respect for his moral stances and Welsh consciousness. He died on 28 February 1961 and is buried at Llantarnum Abbey, Cwmbran, Gwent.[20]

Bishop McGrath.

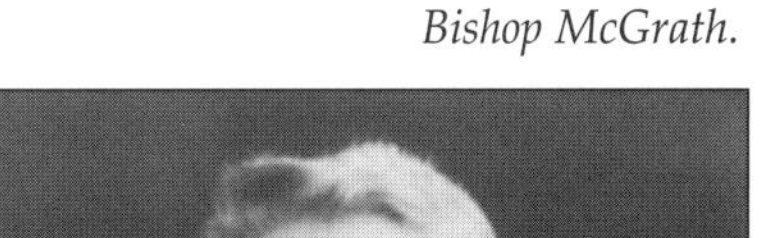

He was succeeded by **Daniel Joseph Hannon**

Bishop Hannon.

(1941–6) as fourth Bishop of Menevia. He was born in Rotheram, Yorkshire on 12 June 1884. The family moved to Cardiff, where he entered St Joseph's College. He studied for a time at the English College, Valladolid, but completed his studies at Oscott where he was ordained priest on 22 September 1907. He did two years further study at the Beda College, Rome.

He was a curate at St David's, Cardiff from 1909. In 1919, he became secretary to Archbishop Bilsborrow, OSB, and became a canon of the new chapter in 1920. In 1921, he became parish priest of St Paul's in Cardiff and the following year, he became Administrator of the Cathedral in Cardiff. He gave a strong lead to his flock encouraging them to become involved in politics, civic affairs and Catholic Action, and he was chaplain to the Catholic doctors and to the Knights of St Columba. He felt the disunity of the Christian churches very keenly and was a competent linguist, speaking Spanish, Italian and Welsh fluently.

From 1930, he was Canon Theologian of Cardiff Archdiocese and in great demand as a preacher. In 1937, he became parish priest of St Joseph's, Penarth and, following the death of Archbishop Mostyn, he was elected Vicar Capitular. He was consecrated as Bishop of Menevia at St Mary's pro-Cathedral, Wrexham on 1 May 1941. During his time as bishop, the war brought a great influx of evacuees into many parts of north Wales and he was responsible for providing for the education and religious needs of the many Roman Catholics from Merseyside and elsewhere. He died at Bishop's House, Wrexham on 26 April 1946 and is buried in Wrexham cemetery.[21]

His successor was **Bishop John Edward Petit (1947–72)**. He was born at Highgate in London on 22 June 1895 and educated at the English College, Vallodolid, Spain and St Edmund's College, Ware and ordained for the diocese of Brentwood on 9 May 1918. He then attended Christ's College, Cambridge, graduating with an MA in 1921 and was then a curate at St Anne's, Victoria Docks. By 1923, he was in charge of Our Lady's Maldon, Essex until the following year, when he returned to Valladolid as Vice-Rector, remaining until 1930. He then took charge of the new parish of Holy Family, Dagenham and the following year, he was appointed to St Edward's, Grays. In 1934, he was appointed Master of St Edmund's House, Cambridge, the house of studies for diocesan clergy. He was to remain until 1946, when he became first Rector of St Hugh's Junior Seminary, recently established at Tollerton, Nottingham. Instead of proceeding with this course of action, he found himself called to be Bishop of Menevia.

Bishop Petit.

He was consecrated at the church of Our Lady, Star of the Sea, Llandudno on 25 March 1947. He, like his predecessors, lived in Wrexham, occupying the see for twenty-five years. During this time, the Catholic Church grew and developed, increasing from 20,000 in 1947 to 39,000 by 1972, being due largely to the greater mobility of the population , many Catholics moving into north Wales from other parts of Britain, especially nearby Merseyside.

Bishop Petit had spent most of his life in the field of education and in Menevia, one of his main priorities was the provision of schools for Catholic children. Of a strongly practical turn of mind, he was fearless in the face of a hostile audience, as when he put the case for Catholic schools to the local authorities. Many Catholic children owe him a huge debt in carrying through his plans for Catholic education. He was also responsible for inviting into the diocese the Little Sisters of the Assumption in 1958, who moved into Oteley House in Wrexham. Their work was to help poor families in a practical way and from the 1960s, the Little Sisters became a familiar sight about the town.

In October 1965, Bishop Petit, by now seventy-years of age and having had a serious illness, asked that an auxiliary bishop be appointed to help him. The Rev. Langton Fox, Rector of St John's College, Wonersh was appointed, being consecrated on 16 December 1965. He was given responsibility for the spiritual welfare of the southern part of the diocese, being based at Llanelli. In due course, when Bishop Petit retired, on 19 July 1972, he succeeded him as Bishop of Menevia, being translated to the diocese on 27 June 1972. Bishop Petit, despite being ill, celebrated his Episcopal Silver Jubilee on 25 March 1972. He died on 3 June 1973 and is buried at Pantasaph.[22]

Bishop Langton Fox, DD, (1973–81), sixth Bishop of Menevia, was born on 21 February 1917 at Golders Green, London. His father, Claude, had served in the Australian forces in the First World War and became a Catholic. After the war, the family was reunited in Australia and Langton and his mother were received into the Church in Brisbane on 5 November 1921. After beginning his education in Australia, on settling in England, he attended the Xaverian College in Brighton and at St Joseph's College, Mark Cross, Sussex and studied for the priesthood at St John's Seminary, Wonersh. He was ordained priest on 30 May 1942. He joined the staff at Wonersh, before going to Maynooth in Ireland for further studies, being the first Englishman to gain his DD there. He then taught at Wonersh for ten years and worked for the Catholic Missionary Society, 1955–9, after which he became parish priest of Chichester. Then, he again returned to Wonersh, this time as Rector, but after only a few weeks, he was appointed to be Auxiliary Bishop of Menevia, being consecrated on 16 December 1965. He succeeded Bishop Petit as Bishop of Menevia in 1972.

Bishop Fox.

Bishop Fox was President of the Commission for Priestly Formation, and served on the Commissions for Ecumenism, Liturgy and Theology. He was also a member of the Papal Secretariat for the Unity of Christians. He was very active in the Charismatic Movement, especially in Wales and was appointed Ecclesiastical Assistant to Charismatic Renewal.

He was always keen to encourage putting into effect the new insights of the Second Vatican Council and entering fully into the spirit of ecumenism, encouraging his flock to take part in ecumenical activities.

While taking part in the Welsh National Pilgrimage to Lourdes in 1979, he suffered a stroke and was incapacitated for the rest of his life. On 5 February 1981, he resigned from the diocese. On his death on 26 July 1997, Archbishop Ward said of his last years, 'Bishop Fox was a wonderful example of coping with illness and he always kept cheerful.'[23]

Bishop John Aloysius Ward, O.F.M. (Cap.), (1981–3), had grown up in Wrexham, where he attended St Mary's School and was an altar server at the Cathedral. He entered the Capuchin Franciscan order and spent his noviciate at Pantasaph, where he spent the first seven years of his priestly life, having been ordained in 1953. During this time, at Bishop Petit's request, he undertook Travelling Mission work, bringing the Mass and the sacraments to Catholics who lived far from any church. From 1960 to 1966, Fr. Aloysius was Guardian and Parish priest at Peckham in Southwark Diocese and from 1966 to 1970, he was Director of Vocations for the Capuchin Fathers. In 1970, he was elected Provincial, but after six months, he became Assistant General of his order. He held this position for ten years until, on 1 October 1980, he was ordained Co-adjutor Bishop, with right of succession to Bishop Fox, who was now experiencing poor health. On the resignation of Bishop Fox in January 1981, Bishop Ward became the seventh Bishop of Menevia and took up residence in Bishop's House, Sontley Road. It was during his time as bishop, that Pope John Paul II made his historic visit to Britain and Catholics from all corners of Wales converged on Cardiff to celebrate the visit. Archbishop Murphy of Cardiff and Bishop Ward welcomed the Pope on behalf of the Roman Catholics of Wales. In May 1983, it was announced that Bishop Ward would succeed the retiring Archbishop of Cardiff, a position he held until 2000.[24] He died on 27 March 2007.

Bishop Ward.

Bishop James Hannigan (1983–94), was ordained eighth Bishop of Menevia on 23 November 1983. Mgr Hannigan had spent most of his priestly life working in the Curial Offices at Bishop's House, as Bishop's Secretary, Diocesan Treasurer and Secretary to the Diocesan Education Commission etc, so that he knew the diocese intimately. Whilst he was bishop, the Catholic dioceses in Wales were reorganised for greater efficiency and convenience, so that where there had been two dioceses, Cardiff and Menevia, there was to be formed a third diocese made up of territory from both and to be known as Menevia. North Wales, formerly part of Menevia, was to become the diocese of Wrexham. Bishop Hannigan was translated to his new diocese on 24 March 1987. He served with distinction on various

Bishop Hannigan

national education committees and he was Chairman of the Catholic Education Council, 1985–91. He was an indefatigable worker and when his health deteriorated, despite pleas to slow down, he did not spare himself. In 1994, he had to enter hospital for an operation on his heart and he died there on 6 March.[25]

Bishop Edwin Regan, (1994 to date), succeeded Bishop Hannigan and was ordained Bishop of Wrexham in St Mary's Cathedral on 13 December 1994. Born in Port Talbot, West Glamorgan, on 31 December 1935, Bishop Regan had spent most of his priestly life in the Archdiocese of Cardiff. He studied for the priesthood at St John's, Waterford and was ordained on 5 July, 1959. He served for a few months at Pontypridd, before being appointed to St Joseph's, Neath. In 1966, he was sent for further studies to Corpus Christi College in London and on his return, he was charged with setting up the Diocesan Catechetical Commission of which he was Chairman. In the early days, he ran the Commission from the Convent in Porthcawl, where he also served as chaplain. In 1971, he was appointed Administrator of the Cathedral. Since becoming Bishop of Wrexham, he has become Chairman of the Schools Committee of the Catholic Hierarchy of England and Wales. He was also a member of the steering group for ICONS, a Secondary Schools programme for religious education. A fluent Welsh-speaker, Bishop Regan involves himself in *Cylch Catholig* and is also active in *Cytun*, the Welsh ecumenical body. As a member of *Dolen Cymru*, he has been concerned with the twinning of Wales with Lesotho. In 2000, he was the inspiration behind Congress 2000, bringing together Catholics from all parts of the diocese to discuss many areas of Catholic life. A memorable Mass in Llangollen marked the Millennium. More recently, in August and September 2006 he undertook a sponsored walk of four hundred and fifty miles, following the old pilgrim route to Compostella, raising £24,000 in aid of the repairs to the spire of the cathedral and the Lesotho Aids Charity.

Bishop Regan.

There has been a Roman Catholic bishop resident in Wrexham since the 1890s. They have come from a variety of backgrounds and have had numerous different gifts but between them they have all served north Wales well, and Wrexham in particular, for over a hundred years.[26]

Priests

It was **Fr. John Briggs**, a Lancashire man, who came into north Wales from Chester in the early 1820s to see if he could discover any Catholics and, finding a number in Wrexham and the surrounding district, thus started the mission there. At the time, he was in charge of St Werburgh's, Chester, where he served from 1818 to 1833. He then became President of the northern college of Ushaw until 1836. In 1836, he was appointed Vicar Apostolic of the Northern District and, in 1840, Vicar Apostolic of the Yorkshire District. At the Restoration of the Hierarchy in 1850, he became Bishop of Beverley, ruling the see until just before his death in 1861. The first priest after Fr. John Briggs to celebrate Mass in Wrexham was a **'Mr Fleetwood'** in 1829.[27]

Clergy and servers at the enthronment of Bishop Vaughan, 1926. Back row L–R: Fr. Lofthouse; J. Mitchell; Eric McMahon; Fr. Fitzgerald; Revd Dr Baron; –?–; -?–. Middle row: Fr. A. Pozzi; Fr. F. Cashman; Fr. Brunter; Fr. McGrath; Fr. O'Rourke; Fr. Moran; Fr. Daniel; Fr. J. Pochard. Front row: Fr. Diego; Canon Thompson; Canon Quinn; Canon Nightingale; Bishop Vaughan; Canon Finucane; Canon W. B. Jones; Fr. Hope; Fr. Furniss.

Rev. D. L. Morton, is said to have been the first priest resident in Wrexham in 1831. He may have been the priest of that name educated in Carlow, Ireland, but no more is known about him.[28] Then, in 1833, **Rev. John Wilcock**, successor of Rev. J. Briggs at Chester, visited Wrexham Mission, but he died of fever caught at Nantwich, which he also attended from Chester.[29]

Rev. John Tobin 1833–7 and again from 1840–7.

Rev. John Collins, 1837–9. 'He is spoken of as a hardworking priest and as well-suited to the times. He would walk many miles to administer the sacraments, even to Oswestry about 20 miles hence.'[30] 'In 1839 Rev. John Collins celebrated the first Mass here in a room of the White Lion Inn in Willow Street. This was on Market Day and orange boxes were used to form an altar. Sometimes about 40 people were present.'[31]

Rev. Joseph Hely, 1839–40 'is described as a young and active priest.'[32]

Rev. John Tobin, 1840–7. 'He was always much respected.' He was born in Ireland. He was ordained in 1832 and was Rector of Wrexham, 1832-36 and 18 October 1840–7, Rector of Bangor, 1847–53, Rector of Shrewsbury 1853–6, Administrator of Shrewsbury Cathedral, 1856–67 and Rector of Plowden, 1867–73. He died on 4 September 1878. It was during his time that Shrewsbury Cathedral was built by Edward Welby Pugin, the same architect who designed St Mary's, Wrexham.[33]

Rev. Joseph Jones, 1847–50, son of Herbert and Mary Jones, he was born in Ysceifiog, Flintshire on 21 May 1800. He had been a Methodist lay preacher, becoming a Catholic in about 1839. He was a bard and published some works in Welsh. He entered All Hallows, Dublin in 1844 and also studied at Quimper, Brittany in 1845. He was ordained at All Hallows on 2 August 1845. He became Rector of Abergele 1846–7, Rector of Wrexham and

Mold 1847–50, Rector of Brecon 1850–1, curate at SS Philip and James, Stockport 1851–3, Rector of Bangor 1853–9, Rector of Dukinfield 1859–63, Rector of Holyhead 1863–5, Rector of Seacombe 1867–8, Rector of Welshpool 1869–71. He died in 1871.[34]

Rev. Lewis Havard, 1850. He was born in Breconshire in 1809 and was a Welsh-speaker. 'Brecon depended almost entirely on the Havard family, which provided the Church in these parts with several priests.'[35] He was educated at the English College, Lisbon and ordained in 1837. He died in 1871.

Rev. John Coulston, 1851–3 was the son of John and Margaret Coulston (Walmesley) of old Catholic stock and was born on 7 January 1822 in Lancaster. He was educated at Ushaw, 1836–47 and ordained there by Bishop Riddell on 9 May 1847. He became curate at St Augustine's, Granby Row, Manchester 1847–8 and curate at St Chad's, Manchester 1848–9. He was Rector at St Marie's, Bury 1849–50 and St Werburgh's Birkenhead 1850–1. He became Rector of Wrexham 1851–3, Rector of St Michael's, Stockport 1853–7, chaplain Lingdale House, Claughton [FCJ] 1857–63, Rector of Upton 1863–6, Rector of Welshpool 1866–8, Rector of Oswestry 1868–71, Rector of Wilmslow 1871–89. He died on 4 June 1889 and is buried in Lancaster Cathedral cemetery. There is a Coulston chapel in Lancaster Cathedral.[36]

Rev. John Reah, 1853–7. He was born at Hilltop, Esh, County Durham near Ushaw College on 1 July 1820 and educated at the English College, Lisbon 1835–44. His first appointment was as curate of St Joseph's, Liverpool, 1844–5. He was the first resident priest in Bollington 1845–6, then he was curate at St Mary's Mulberry Street, Manchester 1846–8 and Rector of Hyde 1848–53. He was made a canon in 1852 and was appointed as Rector of Wrexham 1853–7. He retired to Ringwood Road, Poole, Dorset where he died of consumption on 19 December 1859. He is buried in Poole Cemetary. The building of St Mary's, Wrexham was started in his time.[37]

Rev. James Ward, 1856. Nothing seems to be known about him. He was possibly a curate.

Canon Edward Francis Browne, 1857–72, was the son of Edward and Alice Browne (Greehalgh), born in Blackburn on 9 September 1816. He was educated at Sedgley Park in 1829 and the English College, Lisbon 1829–39. He was ordained in 1839 and became Rector of Minsteracres 1839–42, Rector of Great Eccleston in the Fylde 1842–6, Rector of St Werburgh's, Birkenhead 1846–57 and Rector of Wrexham, 1857–72. He died on 17 July 1872, aged 56, and was buried on the right hand side of the walk leading from Regent Street to the east door of the church. In his time, the Brook Street schools were built. He had five brothers who were priests.[36]

Canon Ambrose Lennon, 1872–6, son of Ambrose and Catherine Lennon (Waterhouse) was born in Bolton on 11 February 1811. He was educated at Ushaw 1823–34 and ordained there on 14 March 1835. He was a curate at St Anthony's, Liverpool, Rector of Liscard, 1843–68, Rector of Newport in Shropshire, 1868–72 and Rector of Wrexham, 1872–6. He was made a canon in 1852 and Vicar General in 1867. He died on 29 March 1876, aged 66, and was buried at Liscard Roman Catholic Church.[39]

Canon William Hilton (1876–83) was born in Liverpool on 4 November 1824, the son of Henry and Susanne (Groatson). He was educated at the English College, Lisbon and ordained on 21 December, 1850. He was the first priest to be ordained for the newly-formed Shrewsbury diocese. After ordination, he was on the staff of the secular boarding school, Lisbon, where he was made Procurator in 1854 and Vice-Rector in 1856. He was chaplain at

Talacre Hall, Flintshire from 1857 to 1858, when he became Rector of Bollington. From 1860–7, he was Rector of St Peter's, Stalybridge and Rector of Hooton 1867–77. He was Rector of Wrexham from 1877–83. He was made a canon in 1864, Vicar General in 1876 and Provost in 1877. From 1883–1911, he was President of the English College, Lisbon, where he was considered to be outstanding. He died on 26 August 1911 and is buried in Lisbon.[40]

Canon Henry Hopkins, (1883–95) was born in Birmingham on 9 October 1817, son of William and Winifred Hopkins (Pratt or Bratt). He was ordained at Mount St Bernard's for the Rosminians, on 18 September 1847. He taught at Ratcliffe College, 1847–9, and then became Rector of St Mary's Newport, Monmouthshire 1849–56. He was on the staff of Ratcliffe from 1856 to 1860 and Rector of St Marie's Rugby 1860–1. In 1861, he joined the Diocese of Shrewsbury, becoming curate at St Peter's, Stalybridge and then Rector at St Werburgh's, Chester 1861–5, curate at Shrewsbury Cathedral 1865–7 and Administrator of the Cathedral 1867–9. He then became the Rector of Hyde 1869–79, Rector of SS Philip and James, Stockport 1879–83, Rector of Wrexham 1883–95, and Rector of Wilmslow 1895–1900. He became a canon in 1889 and died on 16 March 1900.[41]

Monsignor Edward Henry Slaughter, (1896–1900) was the son of Edward and Frances Slaughter (Mostyn) and was born in Duchess Street in the district of All Souls, London, Middlesex on 13 January 1846. He was educated at Sedgley Park and Oscott 1857–9, Ushaw 1859–64, the English College, Rome 1864–5 and Ushaw again 1865–9. He was Bishop's Secretary until January 1871. He was ordained at Shrewsbury Cathedral on 24 January 1869 and was appointed a curate at St Laurence's, Birkenhead 1870–2 and Rector of Our Lady's, Birkenhead 1872–91. He became Rector of Plowden 1891–5 and Rector of St Mary's Wrexham 1895–1900. During this time, he was Secretary to Bishop Mostyn who was his cousin. Having been orphaned as a child, they were brought up together. He wrote a two volume history of the diocese of Shrewsbury, but for some reason, he never completed the Welsh section. In the Diocesan Archives at Wrexham, are answers to a questionnaire sent out by the bishop requesting information from the clergy regarding the history of their missions. Presumably these papers were intended as a basis for the missing Welsh section.

As well as writing history, Mgr Slaughter (he was created a Monsignor in 1888) was also an active man, for in 1895, he gave a lantern lecture to the members of the Catholic Young Men's Society, when he talked about a trip to the Alps and his ascent of Mont Blanc. He was also said to have had a remarkable relationship with the poor, who never forgot his kindness.

It was in 1898 that the Welsh Vicariate had been raised to the status of a diocese and granted the old pre-Reformation title of Menevia, of which Bishop Mostyn became first bishop and Mgr Slaughter the first administrator of St Mary's Church. He 'took up with much zeal the work of supplementing the requirements of the pro-Cathedral by erecting a finely finished new altar. The design for this altar as also for those for the Bishop's throne and pulpit were drawn by Mr Peter Paul Pugin.'

He retired to Rome in 1900 and moved to Brighton in 1902. The following year, he entered a home for sick and retired priests in Southampton, where he died on 6 August 1904.[42]

Canon William H. Bickerton-Jones 1900–03 was a Welsh-speaking convert, a Montgomeryshire man, born in Welshpool in 1863. His father was a well-known solicitor. He was educated at Oswestry Grammar School and at Christ's College, Brecon under Dr Edward Lloyd, later Bishop of Bangor. Eventually, he qualified as a solicitor, with plans to join his father's practice, but he was received into the Catholic Church in his mid-twenties, altering the course of his life. He thought of becoming a Jesuit entering St Beuno's for a time. He then studied at Oscott, and was ordained in 1896, the first priest to be ordained for the Welsh Vicariate. A fellow student at Oscott was Ambrose Moriarty, who was from Stockport and was later to become Bishop of Shrewsbury. They became life-long friends and at his request, Canon Bickerton-Jones was buried near to him in the cemetery at Shrewsbury.

Canon Bickerton-Jones.

He served the parishes of Pembroke Dock, Tenby and Aberystwyth before coming to Wrexham in 1900. He was asked to open the new parish at Prestatyn in 1903. He became a canon in 1920, but resigned in 1928. He was a very active man and had a talent for music, playing both the piano and the cello. He was a keen angler and golfer and was also interested in literature, history and archaeology. He died, aged 67, on 13 January 1930.[43]

Very Rev. Provost John E. Quinn (1903–13) was born on 6 September 1872 in Cheltenham. He was educated at Douai, where he was a Benedictine novice. He then went to St John's, Waterford and was ordained in the Cathedral there on 19 June 1898 (or 10 August 1898). He served in Pembroke Dock, Wrexham, Bangor, Rhyl and Colwyn Bay. He died on 8 January 1951.[44]

Monsignor George Nightingale(1913–47) was born in Rotherham, Yorkshire on 20 March 1871. He was educated at Valladolid, where he was ordained on 16 August 1896. He first served at St David's, Cardiff, as a curate, then Mold, Talacre, Haverfordwest and Fishguard before coming to the pro-Cathedral as Administrator in 1913, a post he was to hold for thirty-four years. His work in the diocese included being Secretary to Bishop Mostyn and he was a Trustee of the diocese. He was made a canon in 1916, Vicar General in 1921, Provost in 1924 and Domestic Prelate to the Pope (Monsignor) in 1927. He was Vicar Capitular in 1935 and 1940, while the see was vacant.[45]

Monsignor Nightingale.

Canon Adolph Andrew Richard Evans (1947–82) was born on 9 August 1905 in Aberystwyth. He studied for the priesthood at the English College, Valladolid, Spain. He was ordained at the Bishop's Palace in Palencia, Spain on 21 May 1932. His first appointment was to Llanelli, where he remained for three years before coming to Wrexham as assistant priest at the pro-Cathedral and secretary to the newly appointed bishop, Michael McGrath. In 1939, he was appointed to Welshpool, where he remained until, early in 1944, he became an army chaplain. In 1947, he replaced Mgr Nightingale as Administrator of the pro-Cathedral and was made a canon. He remained in this post for over thirty years until he became ill in early 1982 and died on the 15 April of the same year. Canon Evans was a gifted

Canon Evans.

man. Children at St Mary's School enjoyed his sketches on the blackboard, when he visited the school. Frank More remembered him being 'very popular with the youngsters and loved their company.' He was very fond of music and on Sunday evenings before Benedicton he would have a spell on the Cathedral organ. *Finlandia* was one of his favourite pieces. Mgr [later Bishop] Hannigan referred at Canon Evans' funeral to 'his ever present smile, his patience and his manners which were to so many of us an anchor in our everyday lives.'[46]

Canon Cyril Andrew Schwarz (1982–9) was born in Holywell on 22 March 1923 and was educated at St Winefride's Primary School, Holywell, Cotton College, St Mary's, Aberystwyth and Upholland. He was ordained in Holywell on 1 June 1947. He served as Assistant at the Cathedral from September 1947 to July 1952. He was a great organiser. It was during this time that he formed the Bishop's Own Scout Troup, remaining its active chaplain until his last illness. This led to the pantomimes and gang shows. He was the prime and diligent worker in the founding of the Men's Club, also in the 1950s. He was Parish Priest of Buckley, July 1952 to September 1957 when he moved to Llangollen. With the men of the parish, he converted an ironmonger's shop into the Church of the Holy Cross, which we see today. He was also Diocesan Chaplain to the Arch-Confraternity of St Stephen for altar-servers. He became Administrator of the Cathedral in 1982. He died on 13 September 1989.[47]

Canon Schwarz.

Canon Bernard Morgan (1989–99) was born in Dublin on 4 December 1938. He was educated by the Christian Brothers there and at St Patrick's College, Thurles, Ireland. He was ordained at Thurles Cathedral, Tipperary on 10 June 1972. Shortly afterwards, he left Ireland to take up his first appointment as curate in Rhyl in 1972.

Canon Morgan.

In 1975, he moved to Llanelli and a year later, he became assistant priest at the Cathedral. He then became parish priest at Ruabon in 1983. On account of Canon Schwarz's illness, he served as acting administrator at the Cathedral in 1989, until the death of Canon Schwarz, when he became Administrator, serving in the post until 1999, when he moved to Bangor. He was involved in Charismatic Renewal and served on both the Diocesan and National Service Teams for Catholic Charismatic Renewal. He was an ex-officio trustee of the diocese for the ten years he was at the Cathedral and continued for some time afterwards.[48]

Father Brignall.

Fr. Peter Brignall, (1999–) the present dean of the Cathedral, was born in Whetstone, London on 5 July 1953. His parents were Charles and Marie Brignall. His early education was at Sacred Heart Infants School, Whetstone, St Alban's Preparatory School, Finchley and the Challoner School, Finchley.

Later, he attended Barnet College of Further Education. In 1972, he entered Allen Hall and was ordained priest on 18 February 1978 by Bishop Langton Fox at the Church of St Mary Magdalene, Whetstone. As a deacon, he served at Mold for a few months and his first priestly appointment was at Connah's Quay, 1978–9. He then moved to Our Lady, Star of the Sea at Llandudno, undertaking the University Chaplaincy at Bangor, 1979–84, when he was appointed to Haverfordwest for a year. From 1985 to 1989, he was the parish priest of Knighton and Presteigne and from 1989, he was parish priest of St Mary's, Bangor. From 1999 until the present, he has been Dean of the Cathedral, Wrexham. As well as this, he has been editor of the diocesan section of the National Wales Ordo since 1986 and Chair of the Diocesan Liturgy Commission since 1995. He is the Vicar General of the diocese and a trustee. Since 1996, he has been Bishops' Advisor on Health Care Chaplaincy at a national level.

Between 1998 and 2005, he was north Wales representative of the College of Health Care chaplains, and a member of the Professional Registration Group of the College of Health Care Chaplains, the Amicus Union, since 2005.

As befits the dean of the Cathedral, he is keen to see the liturgy, as the worship of the Church celebrated with the greatest possible dignity, embracing all that is human. He feels that prayer, as the raising of the mind and the heart to God, liturgy must touch all of the senses and not just be a perfunctory saying of the words with the minimum of gesture, action or consideration of the environment.[49]

Over the years, there have been about sixty curates in Wrexham parish. For many, it was their first appointment. They all made their mark on the parish and eventually moved on to be parish priests in different parts of the diocese.

There have been two priests who were brought up in Wrexham. **Archbishop John Aloysius Ward** (see entry on p.132) and **Fr. Peter Wilkie**. The latter was born in Oswestry in 1930, the son of Sarah and Ewan Wilkie. In 1937, when the family moved to Wrexham, he attended St Mary's Primary School. Later, he spent some time at St Mary's College, Aberystwyth. At the age of 18, he worked underground at local coal mines for two years to fulfil his National Service obligation.

In 1952, Bishop Petit sent him to study at St Sulpice in Paris, where he received the diaconate. On 15 June 1957, he was ordained priest at St Mary's pro-Cathedral, Wrexham. Later, he was sent to St Mary's Teacher Training College at Strawberry Hill and went on to serve about half of his vocational life in parish work and half in teaching in Catholic colleges. He is currently parish priest in Newtown and, God willing, will celebrate his Golden Jubilee in June 2007.[50]

Deacons

Since the 1980s, there have been two deacons at the Cathedral, **Rev. John Tarbrook and Rev. Iain Cameron**. **Rev. John Tarbrook** was born on 15 September 1941 in Patrickcroft, Manchester and attended Winton Senior School. In 1959, he began training as a nurse at Bridgewater Hospital, Patrickcroft, where he met Janet. They married in 1961 and moved to the Wrexham area, both taking up appointments at the Maelor General Hospital in 1963. Both studied for a diploma in orthopaedics at the Robert Jones and Agnes Hunt Hospital at Gobowen. John continued his career at the Maelor General Hospital and before his retirement, due to illness in 1990, he was Registrar of Project 2000. In September 1981, John was ordained deacon in Ruabon parish, where he had lived for many years. He worked in the parish for some years, until he took up the post of Administrator of the Diocesan Tribunal, working at Bishop's House, Wrexham. For a while, he served in the Cathedral parish, where he had the joy of marrying his son, David and baptising all of his grandchildren. John suffered with very poor health and died on 3 March 2006.

Rev. Iain Cameron was born on 22 September, 1937 in Richmond, Yorkshire. He was educated at St Bede's, Eastbourne, Sussex and the Nautical College, Pangborne, Berkshire. He took up a career in the Civil Service, 1965 to 1997, working in Health and Social Security and War Pensions. He married Vicki on 28 December 1963 and they have five children and nine grandchildren. Iain studied for the diaconate within the diocese and was ordained by Bishop Ward on 1 November 1981, from which date he has served in the Cathedral parish, preaching, taking communion to the sick at home and in hospital. He has also been involved in the RCIA, (Rite of Christian Initiation of Adults), Baptisms and their preparation and funerals. In turn with other deacons, he preached at different parishes in the diocese for the APF (Association for the Propagation of the Faith).[49]

Over many years the clergy in Wrexham have come from a variety of backgrounds, bringing their own individual experience and gifts, each enriching the life of the parish in their ministry of serving Wrexham's Catholic community.

References

1. Quoted in BELLENGER, Dom Aidan, *Fathers in Faith*, 1991.
2. PLUMB, B., *Arundel to Zabi: a biographical dictionary of the Catholic bishops of England and Wales (deceased), 1623–1987*, 1987.
3. PLUMB, op cit.
4. WILLIAMS, J. Anthony, 'Catholic recusancy in Wiltshire, 1660–1791', *CRS*, 1968, p.133.
5. PLUMB, op cit.
6. BELLENGER, Dom Aidan, *Fathers in Faith*, 1991.
7. Holywell Registers, CRS III, 1906.
8. PLUMB, op cit.
9. Downside Archives, Bishop Sharrock's notebook 1798–1800, quoted in BELLENGER, op cit .
10. DOCKERY, J. B., *Collingridge: a Franciscan Contribution to Catholic Emancipation*, 1954.
11. Holywell Registers, CRS III, 1906.
12. Clifton Diocesan Archives.
13. BELLENGER, op cit.
14. PLUMB, op cit.
15. GASQUET, F. A., 'Tomas Joseph Brown – Bishop of Newport and Menevia' in BELLENGER, op cit.
16. PLUMB, op cit.
17. Ibid.
18. Ibid.
19. Ibid.

20. HUGHES, Trystan Owain, 'Archbishop Michael McGrath (1882–1961): a twentieth century St David? The Irishman who came to Wales', in GUY, John R. and NEELY, W. G. *Contrasts and Comparisons: Studies in Irish and Welsh Church History*, 1999.
21. PLUMB, op cit.
22. PLUMB, op cit, Wrexham Diocesan Archives, *Wrexham Leader, Menevia Record*.
23. PLUMB, op cit, *Wrexham Leader, Menevia Record*, 'The Catholic Church in Engand and Wales'– www. catholicchurch. org. uk.
24. Wrexham Diocesan Archives, J. H. 'Bishop John Aloysius Ward, OFM Cap', n.d.
25. Ibid and *Wrexham Leader*.
26. Wrexham Diocesan Archives.
27. Clifton Diocesan Archives & PLUMB.
28. Ibid, List of Missions and Missioners nineteenth c.entury
29. FITZGERALD-LOMBARD, Charles, *English and Welsh Priests, 1801–1914*, 1993.
20. Wrexham Diocesan Archives, Lennon MS, 1874.
31. Ibid.
32. SLAUGHTER, Edward Henry, *History of the diocese of Shrewsbury*, 1886 and 1892.
33. Wrexham Diocesan Archives, LENNON MS, 1874, ABBOTT, op cit.
34. ABBOTT, op cit.
35. Ibid.
36. Ibid.
37. Ibid.
38. Ibid.
39. Ibid.
40. ABBOTT, op cit.
41. Ibid.
42. Wrexham Diocesan Archives, Quinn MS, 1903, and ABBOTT, op cit.
43. *Tŷ Duw: House of God – History of SS Peter and Francis*, 2003 and ABBOTT op cit.
44. ABBOTT, op cit.
45. Ibid and Mgr Mulroy's memoirs.
46. *Menevia Record, Wrexham Leader*, parishioners' memories.
47. Diocesan Directory, Wrexham Diocesan Archives, parishioners memories.
48. Canon Bernard Morgan.
49. Father Peter Brignall.
50. Mrs Barbara More, his sister.
51. Revd Iain Cameron.
52. Mrs Janet Tarbrook.

Bibliography

Primary Sources

DENBIGHSHIRE COUNTY RECORD OFFICE

Copy presentment containing names of Popish Recusants in Wrexham parish [18th c] DD/DM/228/14.

Copy of address to the King concerning the proposed Catholic Bill, 1807, BD/A/70.

St Mary's R.C. School Log Books, 1908-52, DRO/ED/MB/101/7.

St Mary's R.C. School Managers' Minutes 1903-6, DRO/ED/MB/101/7.

FLINTSHIRE COUNTY RECORD OFFICE

Quarter Sessions 12 Jan 1792.

NATIONAL LIBRARY OF WALES

Visitations 1841.

Wrexham Parish Vestry Minutes, 20 April 1825 PD/101/260A.

DIOCESE OF CLIFTON ARCHIVES

Briggs letters.

DIOCESE OF LEEDS ARCHIVES

Briggs letters.

DIOCESE OF SHREWSBURY ARCHIVES

Letter from Bishop Brown to Bishop Briggs, 16 May 1841.

DIOCESE OF WREXHAM ARCHIVES

Lennon MS, Quin MS, John Hugh Jones MS.

BIRMINGHAM CITY ARCHIVES

Hardman Collection: Business Records of John Hardman & Co, stained glass manufacturers and ecclesiastical metalworkers.

CENSUS 1851

WREXHAM TOWN CENSUS, 1841

HOLYWELL REGISTERS

ST MARY'S PARISH REGISTERS 1828-

ST MARY'S SCHOOL LOG BOOKS 1952-

Books

ABBOTT, Canon E. Maurice, *To Preserve Their Memory, Shrewsbury Diocesan Priests (Deceased), 1850–1995.*

Anon, *The Martyrs of England and Wales, 1535–1680*, C.T.S., 1985

Anon, *The Holy Family Sisters in Wrexham, 1879–1979*, 1979.

ANSTRUTHER, G., *The Seminary Priests, 1558–1800*, 4v., 1968–77.

ATTWATER, Donald, *The Catholic Church in Modern Wales*, 1935.

BECK, G.A. (ed.), *The English Catholics, 1850–1950*, 1950.

BELLENGER, Dom Aidan, *English and Welsh Priests, 1580–1800*, 1984.

BELLENGER, Dom Aidan, *Fathers in Faith: the Western District, 1688–1988*, 1991.

BOSSY, J., *The English Catholic Community, 1570–1850*, 1977.

CATHOLIC RERCORD SOCIETY, various volumes.
CLARK, George T., *Report to the General Board of Health on a further inquiry as to the boundaries which might be most advantageously adopted for the borough of Wrexham*, 1851.
CLEARY, J. M., *A Checklist of Welsh Students in the Seminaries*, Cardiff, 1958.
DICKENS, A. G., *The English Reformation*, 1964.
DOCKERY, *Collingridge: a Franciscan Contribution to Catholic Emancipation*, 1954.
DODD, A. H. (ed.), *A History of Wrexham*, 1957.
The Industrial Revolution in North Wales, 1950.
DUFFY, Eamon, *The Stripping of the Altars: Traditional Religion in England, c.1400–1580*, 1992.
ELLIS, T. P., *The Catholic Martyrs of Wales, 1535–1680*, 1933.
FITZGERALD-LOMBARD, Dom, *English and Welsh Priests 1801–1914: a working list*, 1993.
FOLEY, H., *Records of the English Province of the Society of Jesus*, 7v and addenda, 1877–83.
HAIGH, C., *The English Reformation Revised*, 1987.
English Reformations: Religion, Politics and Society Under the Tudors, Oxford, 1993.
H.M.S.O., *Royal Commission on the State of the Irish Poor in Great Britain*, 1836.
HOLMES, Derek, *More Roman than Rome: English Catholoicism in the Nineteenth Century*, 1978.
HUGHES, P., *The Reformation in England*, 3v, 1950–4.
Rome and the Counter-Reformation in England, 1942.
KIRK, J., *Biographies of English Catholics in the Eighteenth Century*, 1909.
McGRATH, P., *Papists and Puritans under Elizabeth I*, 1967.
MAGEE, B., *The English Recusants: Burns, Oates and Washbourne*, 1938.
MATHEW, D., *Catholicism in Engand, 1535–1935: portrait of a minority, its culture and tradition*, 1936.
The Celtic Peoples and Renaissance Europe, 1933.
NEALE, J. E., *Queen Elizabeth*, 1948.
NORMAN, E., *Roman Catholicism in England from the Elizabethan Settlement to the Second Vatican Council*, 1986.
O'DAY, R., *The Debate on the English Reformation*, 1986.
O'LEARY, Paul, *Catholicism and the Irish in Wales in the Nineteenth Century*.
PALMER, A. N., *A History of the Town of Wrexham*, 1893.
PLUMB, B., *Arundel to Zabi: a Biographical Dictionary of Catholic Bishops of England and Wales (deceased), 1623–1987*, 1987.
RICHARDS, T., *Religious Developments in Wales (1654–1662)*, 1923.
RODERICK, A. J., *Wales Through the Ages*, 1959 and 1961.
SCARISBRICK, J., *The Reformation and the English People*, 1984.
SLAUGHTER, E., *History of the Diocese of Shrewsbury*, 1886 and 1892.
THOMAS, D. A., *The Welsh Elizabethan Catholic Martyrs*, 1971.
THOMAS, W. S. K., *Tudor Wales*, 1983.
WARD, B., *The Dawn of the Catholic Revival in England*, 2v, 1909.
The Eve of Catholic Emancipation, 3v, 1911.
WATKIN, E. I., *Roman Catholicism from the Reformation to 1950*, 1957.
WILLIAMS, Glanmor, *Wales and the Reformation*,1997.
The Welsh Church from Conquest to Refortmation, 2nd ed., 1976.
WILLIAMS, W. Alister, *The Encyclopaedia of Wrexham*, 2001.
WILLIAMS, W. Llewellyn, *The Making of Modern Wales*, 1919.
WILMOT-BUXTON, E. M., *A Catholic History of Great Britain*, 1921.

Articles

CLEARY, J. M., 'The Catholic resistance in Wales, 1568-1678', March 1957, pp 111–25.
'Dr Morris Clynnog's invasion projects, 1575-6'. *Recusant History*, v.8, No 6, October 1966.
CLIFTON, R., 'The popular fear of Catholics during the English Revolution', *Past and Present*,52, 1971, pp23–55.

DAVIES, D. Leslie, 'Sir William Lloyd of Bryn Estyn Pt 2', *Denbighshire Historical Society Transactions,* v.26 , pp17–19.

DOYLE, P. J., 'The Giffards of Nerquis', *Flintshire Historical Society Publication*, v.24, 1969.

GRIFFITHS, G. Milwyn, 'Glimpses of Denbighshire in the records of the Court of Great Sessions' *Denbighshire Historical Society Transactions.*

HUGHES, Trystan, 'Archbishop Michael McGrath 1882–1961: a twentieth century St David? The Irishman who came to Wales' in GUY, John and NEELY, W.G. *Contrasts and comparisons, studies in Irish and Welsh Church history*, 1999.

JONES, Emyr Gwynne, 'Catholic recusancy in the counties of Denbigh, Flint and Montgomery, 1581–1625', *Transactions of the Honourable Society of Cymroddorion*, 1945. pp114–33.

'The Lleyn recusancy case, 1578–81', *Transactions of the Honourable Society of Cymroddorion*, 1936.

KENNEDY, T., 'Roman Catholic recusancy in Denbighshire', *Denbighshire Historical Society Transactions.*

'The Edwards family of Plas Newydd in Chirkland', *Denbighshire Historical Society Transactions*, 1992.

MENEVIA RECORD

WILLIAMS, W. Ll., 'Welsh Catholics on the Continent' *Transactions of the Honourable Society of Cymroddorion*, 1901–02.

Unpublished Works

JONES, Peter, 'The Irish in North East Wales, 1851–1881', Ph D Thesis, Manchester, 1999.

Newspapers and Periodicals

The Builder, 1856.
Chester Courant, 1827.
Evening Leader.
Liverpool Daily Post.
Menevia Record.
Recusant History.
Shrewsbury Chronicle.
The Tablet.
Western Mail.
Wrexham Advertiser.
Wrexham Gazette.
Wrexham Leader.